She Loved Everyone But Me

The Dramatic Story of a Mentally Ill Woman and Her Handicapped Daughter

Michael J. Thornton &
Kathleen Thornton Crow

She Loved Everyone But Me

Copyright © 2010 by Michael J. Thornton and Kathleen Thornton Crow

All rights reserved. No portion of this book may be reproduced or transmitted in any form or by any means, electronic or mechanical, including photocopying, recording, or by any information storage and retrieval system without written permission from the publisher, except for the inclusion of brief quotations in a review.

Borderline Publishing LLC
305 N. Steelhead Way
Boise, ID 83704
www.borderlinepublishing.com

ISBN 978-1936408108 (Paperback)

Cover Design by Teaberry Creative Design, Boise, ID

Printed in the United States of America
on post-consumer recycled paper

Dedication

This book is dedicated to mothers all over the world who have made incredible sacrifices to care for their handicapped children. In many cases, these mothers have sacrificed their own personal goals and ambitions to give their children the opportunities other children have.

Acknowledgements

Writing a book is a solitary enterprise for the most part and certainly that was true for us. Though we did derive mutual support from our exchange of memories and ideas, in the end we each labored long and hard to move Mother's and Patty's story from mind to print. Taking the book from these infantile beginnings to a completed project, however, required the invaluable help of three very talented women.

Encouraging us with our first baby steps was Lorry Roberts who listened to our thoughts, read our earliest attempts at chapters and gave us concrete ideas on how to proceed.

Our next major assistance came from our editor, Jean Terra, who made our manuscript appear to be decorated for Christmas with all the red editing marks she liberally sprinkled throughout its pages. Once we recovered from the shock, we had to admit that our project was much the better for her suggested changes.

Another key member of our team was Karen Kiramidjian who worked with us to format our pages into something a publisher might be willing to accept and read.

Finally, we have been blessed by the ongoing support of our spouses, Sheryl and Bill, two salt-of-the-earth Idahoans who have been the catalysts for so much that is good in our lives.

We thank you all.

Prologue

My sister, Kathy, and I wrote this book to document what we thought was an incredible story, a story we had observed firsthand for most of our lives. The relationship between our mother, Eileen Thornton, and our older sister, Patty, was a remarkable example of how much a woman is willing to sacrifice for her child.

Our mother suffered from mental illness most of her adult life. She was manic-depressive or bi-polar, the term that is currently used to describe this condition. Our sister, Patty, was born premature and then was diagnosed with cerebral palsy at three years of age. Mother's life was the day-in-and-day-out struggle of a mentally ill woman trying to do everything possible to alleviate Patty's handicap and to provide her with as normal a life as possible and at the same time to deal with the difficulties created by her own tortured mind.

Kathy and I have tremendous admiration for our mother and marvel at what she was able to accomplish. We are inspired by the sacrifices she made to give Patty as normal a life as possible. The remarkable journey of these two strong women, mother and daughter, spanned 63 years and for Kathy and me it has been an amazing experience reliving it and telling this story of their lives together.

To give our readers a comprehensive look into the lives of these two remarkable women, we had to address other relationships within our family unit, including my own somewhat complicated relationship with our father.

We are not professional authors and this book has primarily

been a labor of love. Our approach might be confusing at times. Kathy and I discovered that we have different writing styles and sometimes one or the other of us has much better recall of specific events. It was surprising to me that despite my extremely close and loving relationship with our mother, Kathy had a much deeper understanding of who this wonderful and complex woman really was. I think Mother and I centered our lives together around her support and fanatical interest in my athletics. We also had that deep bond that I believe many mothers have with their only sons.

In putting the events of our lives on paper, Kathy and I have struggled with what the format should be. Over the seven years we were involved with this project we came to the conclusion that if our effort was going to succeed we would have to take a unique and unusual approach. Rather than trying to condense our thoughts into one voice, we have written complete chapters individually, depending on which one of us had better command of the events covered in a specific chapter.

This book was born out of our strong belief that Mother's and Patty's relationship was so incredible that it had to be documented if for no other reason than for the benefit of the Thornton family who lived it and all their children and grandchildren. If in telling this story we can provide any comfort or insight to other families that are going through a similar life experience—that would be wonderful.

Contents

Chapter One: Riding the Roller Coaster 1
Chapter Two: Guilt 7
Chapter Three: Nature versus Nurture 13
Chapter Four: "Bob, Who?" 23
Chapter Five: When Our Ship Comes In… 33
Chapter Six: Mom's 1952 Breakdown—
    An Indelible Memory 43
Chapter Seven: Electroshock Therapy in the
    Treatment of Manic-Depressive Illness 51
Chapter Eight: The Bond Of Motherhood
    And Only Sons 57
Chapter Nine: My Dad and I—
    A Complicated Relationship 67
Chapter Ten: Welcome Travelers 83
Chapter Eleven: Life Just Isn't Fair 93
Chapter Twelve: Camarillo State Hospital—
    A Trip Into Hell 103
Chapter Thirteen: What a Difference a Day Makes 113
Chapter Fourteen: Lithium: The Miracle Drug 119
Chapter Fifteen: "Oh, Bosh!" 127
Chapter Sixteen: Queen or Oscar? 139
Chapter Seventeen: Don't Grieve for Me,
    For Now I'm Free 147
Bibliography 157
About the Authors 159

Chapter 1

Riding the Roller Coaster

Bob and Eileen on their wedding day, June 22, 1938

Kathy's Chapter

She Loved Everyone But Me

The downward plunge of the roller coaster ride was about to begin again. We had been on the upward phase for several weeks and now all that lay ahead was the steep, scary, frightening drop.

It was a balmy evening in Southern California in March 1960. Four members of the Thornton family were going for a drive in the family car, a 1956 beige and cream Ford Ranchero pickup. At the wheel was 48-year-old Robert, who in most women's eyes would still be placed in the tall, dark and handsome category. Bob had worked as a stonemason most of his adult life and his work-roughened hands gripped the steering wheel tightly as he drove out of Camarillo and headed down the Pacific Coast Highway.

How many times had he climbed aboard this same frenzied ride? Five? Ten? Bob had lost count. When he first encountered and became entranced by the beautiful blonde with the Monroe-esque figure and sassy personality, he had no inkling of what a chaotic life lay in store for him. Now, as he attempted once more to help this woman he so dearly loved, his mind was preoccupied with the problem of how to bring this current rescue mission to a peaceful conclusion. Would his wife, Eileen, see through this ruse of taking a pleasant evening's drive? Bob remained stone silent throughout this trip, his mind completely absorbed in these turbulent thoughts.

Eileen, on the other hand, was amazingly animated. She was exhilarated by the thought of a nice evening drive. She had always loved the feeling that riding in a car gave her. A tremendous sense of freedom and escape came over her as they sped down the road. Inside a moving car, Eileen felt as if she were in a different world, a world of deliverance from everyday cares, worries and woes. A cocoon of safety enveloped her. She loved it!

Two of their daughters, Colleen and Kathy, accompanied Bob and Eileen that night. They were wedged on the front seat between their parents. Sitting next to the passenger door, Eileen regaled anyone who cared to listen with her embellished version of the day's activities. Beginning with her thoughts on the ordination of women that she had shared with Monsignor Moclair after morning Mass, she went on to the banter she had exchanged with her Camarillo Bakery friends over a cup of tea and a slice of her favorite chocolate whipped-cream cake. By Eileen's account they had come up with some marvelous solutions for many of the problems facing their burgeoning community. Then she detailed the advice she had given on child rearing to Fran, the anxious first time mother of a fussy baby boy. By the time Eileen left her neighbor's home, the baby was happily cooing in his mother's arms.

At times like this, multiple thoughts and ideas bounced off the walls of Eileen's brain in rapid succession. Her mind raced to verbalize them as fast as they were created. It made for sparkling, rapid-fire conversation in which she was the heroine who solved everyone's problems and dazzled them with her intelligence and wit, or so she saw it.

Ten-year-old Colleen sat next to Bob. She was totally befuddled as to why her beloved daddy, who could do no wrong in her eyes, had torn her away from her favorite television program to go on this stupid ride. Weary of her mother's non-stop talking, which she had endured since arriving home from St. Mary Magdalene School, Colleen longed to escape and re-immerse herself in the wonderful world of television, where people seemed so much happier than they were in this confusing world in which she lived. Being the youngest member of the family by eight years, Colleen had not been on this ride as many times as her siblings, Patty, Mike and Kathy had been. She hadn't a clue as to what was going on around her. What she did know was that she didn't like it one bit.

She Loved Everyone But Me

I was the fourth passenger in the car that March evening. An eighteen-year-old freshman at Ventura Community College at the time, I, like Dad, had vivid memories of other similar nights and days of growing tension and disruption. I was very nervous about the final outcome of the evening. I had witnessed the highly-charged conversation of the previous night during which Dad had tried to convince Mother that she was headed once again for the precipice and needed some help to stop the inevitable plunge over the edge. Knowing what was coming that night, I had prayed all day that Mom would respond positively to Dad's pleas but, of course, that was wishful thinking of the rankest order. The emotional confrontation had ended with Mother's storming off to her bedroom, a loud door slam the exclamation point to her anger!

And so, all was going as well as could be expected on this family drive until we arrived in Los Angeles. When we pulled up to a red light and stopped, Mother spotted the much too familiar sanitarium, in her mind the dreaded house of horrors. Memories of the innumerable electro-convulsive shock treatments she had received in this torture chamber flooded her mind and sent chills up her spine.

"Bob, how dare you try to deceive me like this! If you think you're putting me in that place again, you've got another think coming," she shrieked as she opened the car door, jumped out and took off running down the boulevard. We three remaining occupants of the car sat stunned by what we had just witnessed. The traffic light changed and the horns blaring from behind us brought us out of our state of shock and into the reality of the situation that faced us.

"Why did Mom jump out of the car, Daddy?" cried Colleen.

"She's afraid, honey, afraid of that building over there, afraid the doctors will hurt her."

"What are we going to do now, Dad?" I asked.

"See that police car over there. I'm going to ask those officers to help us."

And they did. After Dad explained to them that his wife suffered from manic-depressive illness and needed the help the sanitarium could offer, the policemen went after Mother in their patrol car. The three of us followed in the Ranchero. The officers convinced Mother to come with them and before long Dad was accompanying his defeated and sobbing wife into the sanitarium.

The policemen wanted assurance from the administrator that Dad's description of the situation was legitimate and that Mother had indeed been a patient there before. Once that was resolved, the officers left with our father's thanks. All that remained was for him to fill out the admission papers.

When he returned to the car, Dad found me hugging and consoling Colleen, who had been totally overwhelmed by the events of the evening. And so, having completed our heartbreaking mission, we headed for home in silence, hoping once again that this most recent hospitalization would result in the successful healing of the woman we had left behind.

Chapter 2

Guilt

Mother and Patty
January 1939

Kathy's Chapter

She Loved Everyone But Me

Guilt was the dominant emotion in my mother's life. This is not just a matter of speculation on my part. Dr. Kenneth Briggs, one of several psychiatrists who helped Mother put her life back together over the years, told me in 1970, "Ignore the words and listen to the music. When your mother is at her most vitriolic is when she is feeling the worst about herself. The woman is riddled with guilt."

The guilt swept over her like a monsoon threatening to drown her completely as she was being transported to Camarillo State Mental Hospital from the private sanitarium the day after her traumatic admission by my father. She had vehemently refused the electroshock therapy treatments, which had seemingly worked well for her in the past, and had demanded to be transferred to Camarillo. After a phone consultation with Dad, the administrator made the necessary arrangements and Mother was on her way. The events of the previous night had brought the manic phase of her current roller coaster ride to an abrupt halt and dumped her in a heap of depression.

As she traveled north on the freeway from Los Angeles to Camarillo, she mentally battered herself about everything that had gone wrong in the last twenty-two years. My oldest daughter is handicapped — my fault! My husband has taken to drowning his sorrows in alcohol periodically — my fault! My family has too often had to cope without a wife and mother — my fault!

She had fought so hard over the years to overcome her guilt by various means including immersing herself in books such as Norman Vincent Peale's *The Power of Positive Thinking*. Now she was tired of it, tired of trying to overcome it, tired of losing to it. No books, no advice, no prescriptions could shake her conviction that the blame for all our family problems should be laid right at

Guilt

her feet. She was too tired and too discouraged even to cry.

Mother had been so excited at the prospect of a new beginning when the family moved in June of 1959 to Camarillo, a small agricultural community located sixty miles north of Los Angeles. The thought of living in a new place where she could start with a clean slate and no one would ever have to know about her health problems had been so appealing. She and Dad had enjoyed an idyllic summer getting acquainted with their new neighbors and spending a good deal of time tending their son, Mike's, lemon grove. Mother joined the Ladies' Auxiliary at the Oxnard Hospital and enjoyed the friendships and feelings of service she derived from volunteering. She and Dad had both taken great pleasure in following nineteen-year-old Mike's success pitching that summer for the Los Angeles Dodgers' farm team in Kokomo, Indiana. His signing in May of 1958 as the first "bonus baby" for the Dodgers after they moved from Brooklyn to Los Angeles had been a tremendous source of pride for Dad and Mom and they followed his career intently. Family barbecues at the lemon grove and leisurely drives to the beach had also been a big part of that summer. Life had been good. Now, it was over.

Once again, Mother was convinced she had ruined everything. Now, everyone in Camarillo would know about her mental illness. The thought of facing those questioning looks and sidelong glances was more than she could bear. The safest approach, she thought, was just to stay away, away from the world that was so condemning of her, away from her family so they couldn't be harmed or embarrassed by her.

The exception to this isolationist thinking was Patty, her eldest daughter. Patty was the reason Mother had demanded to be transferred from the sanitarium in Los Angeles to the Camarillo State Mental Hospital. Patty was the person she most loved and also the person about whom she felt the most guilt. At Camarillo, she could be close to Patty, could look out for her and protect her because Patty herself was currently a patient at the Camarillo State Mental Hospital! Patty's admission there in 1958 had been a crushing blow as well as an on-going source of guilt for Mother.

She found her thoughts going back to the day Patty was born, October 11, 1938. What a nightmare! The day had started out like most others since her marriage to Dad earlier that year. He left after breakfast for his job at the local Texaco gas station and she busied herself cleaning house. About mid-morning the pains started, just light ones at first but they soon became stronger and Mother was frightened. The baby isn't due for three more months so it can't be labor, she thought.

No one had prepared Mother for what to expect from childbirth. My Victorian grandmother had died when Mom was seventeen and had not given her only daughter so much as a minimal "birds and the bees" talk. Mother had no close female relatives and her obstetrician had not been informative. The birthing classes and literature that are so prevalent today were non-existent in the 1930s.

When her water broke, Mother really panicked and called Dad, who in turn called the doctor. The two men arrived at the house simultaneously only to find that Mother had already given birth to a tiny baby girl who, sadly, was very much dead. Mother was still in the throes of labor and so the doctor, thinking that she was trying to pass the after-birth, reached roughly into the birth canal and pulled out a mass that, before long, he realized was another tiny baby. Dad would always think that the doctor's rough treatment of Patty that day is what led to her many health problems. Fighting desperately now to keep this tiny creature alive, the doctor instructed Dad to call an ambulance and soon mother and child were on their way to the hospital where Patty, weighing in at a whopping three pounds, would spend the first three months of her life in an incubator.

This was the beginning of Mother's guilt. For the rest of her life

Guilt

she would wonder and ponder over what she should have done differently to save her first baby from death and her second one from a life plagued with handicaps. Had she done something during her pregnancy to cause the premature births? If she had called the doctor immediately when the labor pains started, would things have turned out differently? Questions that had no definite answers filled her mind and troubled her spirit. From the day Patty came home from the hospital, Mother was a woman obsessed with trying to make up to her for the handicaps she suffered. Eileen Thornton spent the next sixty years of her life doing everything she could possibly think of to make her daughter, Patty's, life as normal as possible.

Chapter 3

Nature versus Nurture

The Mitchell Family
Agnes Domney Mitchell
Jack, Eileen and Frank
1920

Kathy's Chapter

She Loved Everyone But Me

My mother's life presents a wealth of material for the "nature versus nurture" debate. On the nature side of the equation, modern science tells us that manic-depressive or bi-polar illness, as it is currently called, is a result of "biochemical imbalances of neurotransmitters that accelerate dramatic mood shifts." People are born with a genetic predisposition to this illness in much the same way as other people are predisposed to become diabetics. On the nurture side, however, scientists also think that environmental factors can contribute to bi-polar disorder and sometimes trigger some manic and depressive episodes.

In her autobiographical book, *A Brilliant Madness*, actress, Patty Duke, says of herself, "So the recipe was perfect. Start with genetics, add a lot of loss and turmoil. What you end up with is a classic manic-depressive". This sounds like a perfect description of my own mother's life.

Eileen Patricia Mitchell was born in Toronto, Ontario, Canada on August 7, 1912. She was the third child and only daughter of Charles and Agnes Doheny Mitchell. The family were immigrants from England and owned a fish market on Lake Ontario. Mother had no recollection of her father, a man who evidently had a roving eye. By the time Mother was two years old, Grandmother Mitchell had grown tired of her husband's philandering so she packed all of his belongings and deposited them in the front yard of their home on Woodbine Avenue. Shortly after that dramatic confrontation, Charles Mitchell returned to England and was never again to play a part in Mother's life.

As children of divorce often do, Mother came to blame herself for the dissolution of her parents' marriage. Many times during her childhood she heard her mother say, "the marriage started to go bad after Eileen was born." It is very clear to see that the seeds of guilt were planted early in mother's psyche. She came to see herself as the catalyst for unhappiness in Grandmother Mitchell's life. The fact that her mother never showed her the same affection that she showered on Mom's older brothers, Jack and Frank, served to deepen these feelings. She often described Grandmother Mitchell to me as "a very social and gracious person who seemed to love everyone but me."

Mother's chief memories of her childhood were of days filled with lessons: piano, voice, elocution and ballet. She studied them all, much to her chagrin. Her home was the scene of frequent entertaining during which Mother was called upon to display the fruits of her many lessons and then promptly dismissed.

Grandmother Mitchell was very active in the Catholic Church and the parish priest was a regular guest in their home along with numerous other friends. Except for being called upon to entertain these guests, children of the day were to be "seen and not heard," a very difficult restraint for Mother, who always loved to talk. She attended parochial school but did not seem to have fond memories of the nuns who taught her. In her desire to liven up the highly disciplined classrooms, she came in for frequent admonitions of, "Eileen, you'd better mind your Ps and Qs," a rather odd but popular saying of the time.

Mother was generous as a child and loved to do things for her schoolmates. After class she would often take them to Grandmother Mitchell's fish market for a treat of chips. These French fries, as we Americans call them, were wrapped in newspaper in the English fashion and, according to Mother, were absolutely delectable. One generous youthful impulse brought her mother's ire down on Mom's shoulders. She decided after school one day that she had more dresses than she really needed and wouldn't it be nice to share two of them with a couple of friends who were less fortunate than she. Mother took these girls up to her room and instructed them to choose whichever one of her dresses they liked best!

Mother often spoke of the harsh winters in Toronto and the huge accumulations of snow that were so much a part of them. It was not unusual for the snow to reach all the way to the eaves of their home. One of her favorite winter memories was of sledding down hilly Woodbine Avenue. She happily recalled that if she and her friends got a really good start, they could slide all the way to the frozen Lake Ontario. Perhaps it was these frigid winters that led the family to immigrate to sunny Southern California in 1924 when Mother was twelve years old.

Grandmother sold the fish market and the family home and they took off in their vintage 1920s sedan on a leisurely trip across the United States, eventually settling in Inglewood, California. In addition to Agnes Mitchell and her three children, this group of travelers included a man the family called "Uncle Ide", though he was not a blood relative. A butcher by trade with a distinct British accent, he was a permanent and much beloved member of Mother's family. I was told he had been a dear friend of Grandpa and Grandma Mitchell's when they lived in England. When he emigrated from England to Canada, he boarded with my grandparents and never left, even after Grandpa Mitchell did! One wonders if this rather unconventional arrangement for the early 1900s—two unmarried adults living in a home together with three children—contributed to the desire to move somewhere where Uncle Ide could be described as a relative and thus avoid scandal. The Mitchell family plus one took up residence in Southern California during the region's golden days, the pre-smog, pre-freeway, pre-population explosion era when the whole area was noted for its clear, blue skies, warm sunny weather, and clean, sandy beaches.

Mother completed grade school in Inglewood and went on to St. Mary's Catholic Girls' High School. She found the atmosphere there somewhat stifling and soon transferred to Inglewood Union High School where she met her dearest and closest friend, Dorothy Ochs. These attractive young women presented a salt and pepper appearance to the world. Mother was blond, blue-eyed and fair skinned; Dorothy, brunette, brown-eyed and olive-complected. They shared many fun-filled adventures in high school, oftentimes centered around their mutual love of the beach. They were such strong swimmers that their idea of a perfect afternoon was a long, leisurely swim around one of the piers that were an integral part of each Southern California beach town. The swim would then be topped off by lazy hours of sun-bathing on the sandy shore.

Dorothy and Mother also shared a love of horseback riding. One summer day, when I was still in grade school, I was helping Mother clean up the laundry room and, much to my amazement, I discovered the most beautiful brown and cream horseback riding outfit. It was like something out of an English fox hunt, complete with jodhpurs and knee-high riding boots. Questions from me about this outfit led my now forty-something, rather matronly and graying, house-dressed mother into reveries of description about her riding days. Reliving them took her back to a happier more carefree time.

Her favorite story, repeated to me many times over the years, involved herself and her friend, Dorothy. It seems that one day when they were riding along the beach, several undergraduates from the nearby Loyola University found it amusing to spook Mom's and Dorothy's horses. Fortunately, these young ladies were excellent horsewomen and got their horses sufficiently under control to ride straight to the University president's office and report the dangerous mischief of these young men.

Mother was involved in many activities at Inglewood Union High School including the Sentinel Guard of Honor, Speech and Spanish Clubs and swimming. Among the tributes she received from her classmates in her 1929 Annual was the following from

She Loved Everyone But Me

Dorothy: "This last semester has been one of the best times in all my school life and that's because I was friends with you. You have been such a dear girl and one of the things I most like you for is your sincerity and frankness." Her brother, Frank, penned: "To Eileen, a sure panacea for all blues and a girl I'm proud to call sister." Other students commended her for being "a fine speech maker;" for having "charm, brilliance and good looks;" for dancing a "hot Charleston" and for being "smart and keen and the best history student." A fellow Spanish Club member described her as a "baby-faced blond" and "una sympatica senorita." In short, Mother seemed to enjoy high school and appeared to be well-liked by her fellow students.

Mother's teen years were further enlivened by her brothers' penchant for making "bath tub gin", a not uncommon practice during the Prohibition years in America. The completion of a new batch of gin was always the occasion for a lively party with Jack's and Frank's many friends. Mother was particularly fond of her eldest brother, Jack, who was very devoted to her. Her brother, Frank, was a law student and a ladies' man so he had little time for his baby sister.

Mother's graduation from Inglewood Union High School was forever scarred by the tragic death of her Mother the night before the ceremony. Grandmother Mitchell had chronic high blood pressure, which was never brought under control in spite of the ministrations of a heart specialist her son, Jack, had brought down from San Francisco. The night she died Grandmother was headed down the stairs to the basement of the family home when a stroke hit her. She fell down the remaining stairs and never recovered from the combination of the stroke and the fall.

Our knowledge of our mother's life in the years between her high school graduation and her marriage to our dad is somewhat sketchy. She took some classes at U.C.L.A. but never a full slate. She did some modeling for Los Angeles department stores and seemed to enjoy an active social life with many beaus. It was during this period that she had her first "nervous breakdown" as such episodes were called at the time. The diagnosis was manic-depressive illness, a curse that would haunt her for the rest of her life.

She Loved Everyone But Me

Uncle Ide,
1925

Eileen and her dear friend
Dorothy Ochs,
1930

Grandmother Mitchell, Mother and Frank
enroute from Toronto to southern CA,
1924

Chapter 4

"Bob Who?"

Bob
1930

Kathy's Chapter

She Loved Everyone But Me

It's Memorial Day 2000. Here I am at Sunset Memorial Park cleaning my parents' gravestone and decorating it with flowers. Mother wouldn't approve but it comforts me. When I was a kid and we lived in Hawthorne, California, Mom had a dear Panamanian friend, Elisa Pickell, who took the bus daily to visit her husband's grave. She would tote a folding chair and some flowers and sit for a spell talking to "my Carl", pronounced with a rolling Panamanian "r". Mom loved Elisa like a sister but she would often say to me, "Why Elisa puts herself through this ritual on a daily basis is beyond me. If and when something happens to your father, I will talk to him in the comfort of my own kitchen with a nice hot cup of tea to keep me company. After all, Kathy, our loved ones aren't at the cemetery. They're in heaven!"

Once after Dad died, Colleen and I took Mother to the cemetery to see the joint headstone we had chosen for the two of them. She took one look at that stone and skedaddled back to the car. I don't know whether it was seeing her own name on the headstone, along with Dad's, that startled her or if it was her natural aversion to cemeteries that sent her scurrying but when we were all back in the car, she informed Colleen and me in no uncertain terms that if we wanted to visit the cemetery in the future, we could do so without her as she had no intention whatsoever of going back!

Well, back she is and as I look at this marble gravestone with my parents' names on it, I think of how much like oil and water they were. A contentious union was theirs — lots of love but also lots of wrangling. How did these two opposites find each other and fall in love? It's always been a real source of amazement to me.

As Mother tells it, the first time she was aware of Robert James

"Bob Who?"

Thornton was in 1924. She was twelve years old and had just recently emigrated with her family from Toronto, Canada to the Los Angeles area. It was a cool, rainy winter Sunday so Mother had decided to wear her fur coat to church. Now, a fur coat on a young girl was a common sight in Toronto but certainly not in Inglewood, California. As she was walking up the steps into church for Mass that morning she felt something brush against her back. She turned just in time to see Bob Thornton scurrying down the steps to join his laughing buddies, Barney and Bill. It seems they had dared Bob to touch the new girl's coat and determine if it was the "real McCoy". Mother's first impression of our father was that he was "quite handsome with that curly, dark hair but certainly brazen!"

However, Mother's first love in the Thornton family was J. T., our dad's father. After school Mom would often drop by his grocery store, eagerly anticipating his warm greeting. "Is it a sweet you'd be fancying today, Eileen?" he'd ask in his thick Irish brogue. Then he'd give her a piece of candy.

Many's the time Mother would daydream of this caring Irishman, who always had time to talk and a kind word to say, as being her missing father. Sometimes Dad would be at the store and would give her a wink but at this point in her life, she only had eyes for the kindly J.T.

My dad, Robert James Thornton, was born in County Mayo, Ireland, on June 12, 1912. He was the third child and second son of John Thomas Thornton and Mary Tom Cogbill Thornton. The family lived in Ireland until Dad was three years old and then immigrated to Montgomery, Alabama.

As a young child, Dad, who was an animal lover his entire life, had quite a collection of cats. He often told me the story of a trip the family took to his mother's home in Bowling Green, Kentucky. While he was gone, he left the cats in the care of the family handyman, George Washington Thornton. In the early 1900s some blacks were still adopting the last names of the people for whom they worked. It seems that when Grandpa called home to check on things, George said that everything was fine except for one little matter. "Please tell Master Bobby to hurry home and take care of his catses."

The Thornton family, which now included four children, Gerald, Louise, Robert and Marjorie, moved to Inglewood, California in 1919 when Dad was seven years old. They purchased a lovely home on Larch Avenue and also owned the house next door as a rental investment. Grandpa bought a grocery store in Inglewood and that's where he worked until 1928 when he passed away from a liver ailment. Thanks to Grandpa's prudent real estate investments, Grannie, as we called Dad's mother, never had to work or worry about money, even though she lived another twenty-five years after Grandpa died.

Dad came from a very loving but also a very strict family. At the dinner table, if one of the children spoke without being spoken to, he or she received a sharp rap on the knuckles from Grandpa's table knife. Dad worked at his father's grocery store from an early age and when he learned to drive, he made deliveries after school and on Saturdays. He once confided to me that he would often sneak in a quick set of tennis while making his Saturday deliveries.

Dad attended Cathedral Catholic High School for boys and was very involved in sports and other school activities. His high school yearbook said of him: "Robert Thornton, vice-president of the student body, captain of the varsity football team, business manager of the *Chimes* yearbook and other offices too numerous to mention. Bob has everything necessary to make a regular fellow, cheerful disposition, likeable personality, and a handsome countenance. As captain and end of the varsity, a three year man, he was one of the outstanding stars of our championship team. We will always remember you, Bob, as a perfect gentleman."

When Dad graduated from high school in 1931, the United

"Bob Who?"

States was in the midst of the Great Depression so he was unable to attend college as had his older brother, Gerald. Dad went to work as a traveling salesman for a flooring company, selling carpeting and linoleum all over Southern California as well as in the Phoenix, Arizona area. When he was home from the road, he continued to live with his mother.

Mother and Dad dated off and on during their teen years and their early twenties but nothing serious came of their relationship until they were both twenty-five. One night that year Mother received a phone call and when she answered the caller said, "Hello, Eileen, this is Bob."

Her response was, "Bob who?"

Mother confessed to me that she had recognized him right away and her heart was pounding when she heard his voice but after three years with no word, she wasn't going to give him the satisfaction of admitting she knew immediately who it was.

Well, at this stage in their lives it didn't take too many dates for both Mom and Dad to realize that they didn't want to go on living without each other. They decided to elope and keep their marriage a secret. It seems that Grannie did not share Grandpa J.T.'s affection for Mother. Dad figured if he and Mom eloped, that would give him time to soften Grannie up to the idea of their marriage. Dad and his mother were very close and he didn't want to go against her wishes or upset her if he could possibly avoid it.

Pregnancy resolved that little problem and on June 25, 1938, Mom and Dad had their marriage blessed at Mission Santa Barbara with all the Thornton and Mitchell family members in attendance. Dad quit his job with the flooring company and began working at a local Texaco gas station for the grand salary of $30 per month. This was the beginning of a stormy but loving marriage that was to last for 52 years until Dad passed away of heart failure in October, 1990.

My early memories of my dad center around his great joy in

playing with his children. One day when he was entertaining our friends and us by walking across the front lawn on his hands, our neighbor, Linda Dixon, turned to me and said, "I wish I had a playing daddy like yours."

I had always taken it for granted that my daddy spent so much time playing ball, jacks, jump rope and showing off his athletic skills with us kids. After Linda's comment, it dawned on me that the other neighborhood dads were not doing these things. She helped me see how truly fortunate I was to have a "playing daddy." It was easy to think of Dad as just one of us kids as his eyes sparkled with such joy when he was playing with us. I was quite convinced as a child that the song, When Irish Eyes Are Smiling, was written for my dad. His smile could truly "melt your heart away."

She Loved Everyone But Me

Dad (at far left), Gerald, Louise and Marjorie, 1916

Dad at Catalina Island, 1936

Dad with Joe behind him, 1952

Grandpa and Grandma Thornton, 1928

Dad at his Texaco job, 1938

Chapter 5

When Our Ship Comes In...

Kathy, Patty and Mike
1943

Kathy's Chapter

Life was on fast forward for Bob and Eileen Thornton from the time they married in 1938 until they bought their first home at 5008 West 140th Street in Hawthorne, California in 1944. By then they had Patty who was five, Mike who was four and me, Kathy. I was three. Good Catholics that they were, Mom and Dad had become living testimony to the limitations of the "rhythm method" of birth control. I guess I should be grateful.

By this time Patty had been diagnosed with cerebral palsy after three years of visits to multiple doctors and hospitals. Mother had kept telling herself that if she just found the right doctor, he would be able to cure Patty but finally she had to accept the cerebral palsy diagnosis and get on with life.

Mother's days were a challenging blur of activity centered around meeting Patty's many needs as well as taking care of Mike and me and maintaining some degree of order in her cozy little two-bedroom bungalow.

Hawthorne, a small suburb of Los Angeles, is nestled between Manhattan Beach to the west and Inglewood to the east. There were just three homes on our block when my family moved to 140th Street but by the time I was in first grade at St. Joseph's Catholic School, the post World War II baby boom was in full flower and the neighborhood had filled up with homes. Ours was a typical working-class neighborhood with working dads and stay-at-home moms living in two-bedroom, one-bath homes. Our dad was a stonemason; Earl Johnson, who lived next door, was a truck driver; Tim McClendon, three doors up, was in the Navy; and Mr. Dixon, on the other side of us, along with several other neighborhood dads, worked in the local airplane factory. It was the rare home that didn't have two, three or more children. Nightly games of kick-the-can were considered the perfect way to end the day. There were many vacant lots in the area and these afforded us the opportunity to run freely, dig underground forts and fly kites. Our feet, our bikes, our roller skates and the Sunset Stages Bus Line were our modes of transportation as most households had only one car, which the dads drove to work each morning.

Ocean Gate Avenue was the cross street just one-half block away and was aptly named as that's where we caught the bus to escape to leisurely summer afternoons at the beach. Mom would prop Patty up in a U-shaped cushion at the water's edge so the waves could tickle her feet. In our later years, Patty often recounted to me how exciting it was the afternoon a particularly large wave swept up around her cushion and started carrying her out to sea. Our ever-vigilant mother, with the help of a very caring young man, caught her before any harm was done and Patty found the whole experience very exhilarating. She loved to tell the story about the "handsome stranger" who had saved her from drowning. Patty also delighted in helping Mike and me build elaborate sand castles. We would start close around her cushion so she could work on them too and then extend our creations out from there. Summer afternoons at the beach provided many happy memories for us Thornton kids.

The streets in Hawthorne all had sidewalks, which enabled Patty to be wheeled in her chair to just about anyplace the rest of us went. Mother loved to walk so the sight of her and Patty tooling around the neighborhood was a familiar one. Billy's Market, three blocks away, was a frequent destination and, of course, there were numerous stops along the way to visit with neighbors.

St. Patrick's Day was a major holiday in our Irish-Catholic home, not quite up there with Christmas and Easter, but close. The wearin' of the green, the eatin' of the Irish Stew and the singin' of Irish songs were all part of the celebration. Learning all the verses of "McNamara's Band" was practically a rite of passage for a

She Loved Everyone But Me

toddler in our home and we all belted it out loud and clear on St. Patrick's Day along with *When Irish Eyes Are Smiling*, *The Rose of Tralee*, *The Irish Lullaby*, and my personal favorite, *I'll Take You Home Again, Kathleen*. This holiday had special meaning for Patty as St. Patrick was her patron saint. The names we other three Thornton children were baptized with—Michael, Kathleen and Colleen—had a decidedly Irish ring to them too.

Ethnicity and nationality were subjects that were frequently and openly discussed in the 1940s and 1950s. The Southern California of my childhood was a vibrant example of the American melting pot. So many residents were first and second-generation Americans or had come to California from another state that discussing one's background was a comfortable and interesting topic of conversation in our neighborhood. Frequently, after meeting new friends or neighbors, Mother and Dad would sit around the kitchen table and launch into a conversation that went something like this:

"What kind of a name is Turnage, Bob?"

"Sounds English to me, Eileen."

"They say they moved here from Arkansas so if they're originally from England, it must be back a generation or two."

"Well, they seem like pretty nice people even if they are English."

To be English, of course, to my born-in-Ireland dad seemed like a heavy burden for a person to have to carry through life. The Irish and English were still engaged in their extended war and Dad's opinion of the English was definitely influenced by that fact. Being Irish was one of the greatest blessings a person could have, to his way of thinking, and so Ireland and all things Irish were number one in his book. Never you mind that both he and Mother had a smattering of other nationalities in their gene pools, French, German and the much-maligned English among them. As far as Mom and Dad were concerned, they were Irish.

When Our Ship Comes In…

"When our ship comes in" was a frequently used expression in our household. It referred to an improvement in Mom's and Dad's financial situation and was always followed by the most wished-for desire of the moment. Most often it went something like this: "When our ship comes in, we'll take the kids and go to Ireland." A reverie of things they would do there then ensued. On other occasions, the ship would bring a bigger and better house to us. When I was in grade school, I was willing and eager to enter into these exciting discussions. I would get all caught up in the wonderful things that were going to happen when that ship finally docked. As I moved into my more cynical teen years, I began to see these exchanges of my parents as sheer and utter pipe-dreaming. That ship of theirs was never going to find its way into our port! Now, I understand that it was a tool they used to keep hope alive in spite of all the problems they had to face and setbacks they had to overcome. That ship symbolized to Mom and Dad that someday their lives would be better and their dreams would come true.

Another association that was part and parcel of being a Thornton was membership in the Catholic Church. We were all infant-Baptized, First-Confessioned, First-Communioned and Confirmed at the ages the Church deemed appropriate and, by golly, when it came time to marry, a priest better be present. Mike, Colleen and I all went to St. Joseph's Catholic Elementary School and when it came time for high school, Mike was off to Junipero Serra Catholic High School for boys and I to Marymount High School for girls. Sunday Mass was mandatory and when we were students at St. Joseph's we often went to daily Mass. Mike was an altar boy and it always made me proud to see him up on the altar assisting the priest.

Priests were frequent visitors to our home, particularly the assistant pastors, Father Gannon and Father McCarthy. One of the duties of assistant pastors was to visit the sick and, from their point of view, Patty fell into that category so we would oftentimes have white-collared visitors, much to Patty's delight.

Mother and Patty occasionally made trips to the convent to visit the nuns, the Sisters of Providence, who taught at St. Joseph's. They treated Patty like royalty and she loved them all, especially Sister Marie Gerard, the first grade teacher. Many a novena was prayed by these nuns for healing for Patty and they were always hoping that someday she could visit the famous healing shrine at Lourdes in France.

The American institution that is the quintessential manifestation of Irish-Catholicism is Notre Dame University and our whole family were huge Notre Dame fans. The person who first brought us into direct contact with Notre Dame was Sister Angela Clare, the nun who taught Eighth Grade at St. Joseph's and who had Mike and me as students in successive years. (One of my pet peeves in grade school was that all the nuns, after having Mike in class for a year, would take several months to remember to call me "Kathy" instead of "Mike.") Sister Angela Clare was the most devoted Notre Dame fan I have ever personally known. She led a large Notre Dame fan club composed of all her students, who usually numbered about sixty, an unheard-of size in today's classrooms. One of the bulletin boards in the front of the classroom had pictures of the Notre Dame players and chronicled the progress of the "Fighting Irish", as the team is known. Each pupil was assigned a member of the team and as part of our weekly English assignment, we were required to write our player a fan letter. Sister would gather up all the letters, grade them and then ship them off to the University. Believe it or not, the players often responded. This fan club had been going on for so long and with such devotion that a visit to St. Joseph's was part of the itinerary every other year when the Notre Dame team traveled to Los Angeles to play the University of Southern California. My eighth grade year was a travel year for Notre Dame and I will never forget the visit that several of the team members made to our school. We

When Our Ship Comes In…

kids were all dressed up in our Sunday best and the group that greeted the players included my brother, Mike, and all his buddies. Talk about a bunch of excited fans! The sight of those huge fellows just lit up our eyes and our hearts and made us feel pretty special. Thanks to Sister Angela Clare, I still know all the words to the Notre Dame fight song and to this day it has the spark to stir my soul whenever I hear it.

These influences from my parents and teachers instilled in me and my siblings at a young age the concept that it was a real privilege to be both Irish and Catholic!

She Loved Everyone But Me

Mother, Patty and some neighborhood friends enjoying a pony ride on Patty's 8th birthday. Patty is bald from her recent exploratory brain surgery, Oct. 11, 1946

Colleen Therese joined the family on April 10, 1949

Chapter 6

Mom's 1952 Breakdown— An Indelible Memory

Our one and only
Family photo
1952

Mike's Chapter

It was midway through March 1952 and things at the Thornton house in Hawthorne, California, were about to come to a head. The cycle normally took about three months, starting with the manic stage. In some ways Mother was at her best during this phase, very upbeat and seeing the world as a wonderful place unless one of us crossed her.

According to Dr. Max Fink in his book, *Electroshock: Restoring the Mind,* "Mania is an uncommon form of mood disorder. Those afflicted with it are overactive, intrusive, excited, and often belligerent. Many of them believe they have special powers, that they are famous or are related to famous people, and that they can read others' minds. They spend money lavishly. Voices on the radio or television are understood as direct communications. They speak rapidly, and their train of thought is often illogical and confused. They move incessantly, and sometimes write page after page of nonsense. They sleep and eat poorly, have little interest in work, friends, or family, and may require restraint or seclusion. Some are likable when in their manic state; others are angry and frightening."

Mother was an extremely bright person and in the manic state of her illness she took center stage and had a lot to say about many subjects. It was obvious now to those of us who had been through the experience with her before that something was very wrong. She was going too fast and everything was almost too wonderful but in reality, she was losing control. At this point in the cycle of her manic-depressive illness, she was heading down a path that would eventually lead to extreme depression and then a total breakdown.

It was about 9:00 p.m. in the evening and Mother had progressed from the manic stage and she had now arrived at the severe and sometimes suicidal stage of depression.

Our little 1200 sq. ft. 3-bedroom home in Hawthorne, California, was starting to close in on us all. I was 12 at the time and the garage had recently been converted into a family room/bedroom for me while my three sisters, 14-year-old Patricia, 11-year old Kathy and the baby, 3-year-old Colleen, all shared a bedroom on the other side of the house next to Mom and Dad's bedroom. To this day, Colleen doesn't have any recollection of any of these events when this particular breakdown occurred.

We had lived in the little house on 140th Street since I was 4 years old and the saga of the Thornton family was no longer hidden from our neighborhood family. It was a fairly close group of middle-class working people and to some extent we all shared in one another's lives.

During the manic stage of her illness, Mother ran up charge accounts all over town and the bad news typically wouldn't hit the mail box until Mother had been committed to a sanitarium. During this early stage of the illness, she was sometimes euphoric and some of her boundless energy was expended in shopping and walking all over town, kids in tow. In her entire life, Mother never, ever drove a car and we walked everywhere. This was just one of many unique things about our wonderful mother. Walking with her was an experience. You couldn't dilly dally or she would be hollering at you to keep up or you'd lose sight of her altogether. The woman was an Olympic–class walker and her training consisted of dragging us kids all over Hawthorne, three miles to town and three miles back for everything from school supplies to clothes.

Walking was a big thing in Mother's life. I think for her it was extremely therapeutic and the long walks helped her deal with her manic-depressive illness and the stress and frustration of caring for the love of her life, our sister, Patty. Mother's 63-year relationship with Patty is an incredible testimony of the love of a mentally ill

She Loved Everyone But Me

woman for her handicapped child and of the determination of that mother to do everything in her power to make her daughter's life as normal as possible.

The eventual discovery of hundreds of dollars in unpaid bills was just a small part of the incredible burden that Dad had to bear. When things got bad, we would be shipped all over town to stay with different relatives. On two occasions, Kathy and I were put into foster homes. During this March 1952 breakdown, we talked Dad into letting the two of us remain at home. Colleen went to stay with our Aunt Louise and Uncle Emmett. They had a big home in Inglewood and Louise, Dad's sister, was always willing to help. Patty stayed in Los Angeles with our dear friends, the Champommiere family.

Joe Champommiere, a Frenchman, was Dad's partner in the masonry business for many years. Joe had been in the United States for over 30 years but he still sounded as though he had just gotten off the boat. What a great man! And his wife, Clara, was an absolute saint. She was still taking care of foster kids when she was 80 years old. She had had over 100 foster kids live in her home during her remarkable life.

I don't know how Dad did it. In the middle of all the chaos, he never missed a day of work and managed somehow to hold everything together. I regret that while he was alive I never made it a point to tell him of my admiration and great respect for him as a person, for how he maintained his loyalty to a wife who suffered from mental illness throughout their entire married life, and for his concern and love for his four children, one of whom was handicapped and required constant care and attention.

On this March night in 1952, Patty and Colleen had been in bed for a couple of hours. Mother believed that her children should get a good night's sleep and I'm sure the struggle of taking care of a handicapped child all day also had something to do with our going to bed so early.

Mom's 1952 Breakdown—An Indelible Memory

At 14 Patty was beginning to turn into a young woman. Mother's routine was to bathe Patty in the morning, dress her for the day, put her braces on and then lift her into her wheel chair. During the day, Mother put Patty on and off the bed pan. Taking care of Patty's daily needs was like caring for an infant.

Patty was able to feed herself, though, and I think mealtimes were her favorite times of the day. She loved to eat and, as she got older, this proved to be a constant bone of contention between her and Mother as her excessive weight became a problem. It's hard to believe that Patty came into this world weighing just three lbs. She sure made up for that small start in life as she eventually tipped the scales at 170 lbs and she was barely five feet tall. It's almost impossible to describe what Mother did on a daily basis to take care of all of Patty's needs, how her love for Patty fueled her determination to make her walk. Despite all the surgeries, and there were many, and despite the braces on her legs that she wore for many years, and all the prayers that were offered by a lot of people, Patty never managed to walk.

Now, Dad knew that the time had come. He, my sister Kathy and I were having a conversation that evening in the living room. Mother was in the bedroom talking uncontrollably to herself. She was aware that her worst nightmare was being organized and planned.

Dad told us that he had called for the ambulance and that it would be arriving any minute to take Mother to the sanitarium. I think the whole experience is more frightening to me today than it was at the time. We had been through this experience with Mother before and it was as though we almost grew to expect total chaos in our lives.

To Mother, going to the sanitarium meant more electroshock therapy. She had had her first series when she was just 19 years old and she had never forgotten her terror. In the 1940s and 1950s electroshock treatments were thought to be the most successful means of dealing with manic-depressive illness but the procedure at that time was barbaric. Today, in the state of California and most other states, the patient's consent and signature of approval are required before this treatment is undertaken.

Mother finally came out of the bedroom with a wild look in her eyes and, knowing what we were up to, proceeded to give Dad, Kathy and me hell. She was furious and scared to death. As long as I live, I'll never forget the look on her face as she told us that, by God, she was not our mother and didn't ever want to have anything to do with us. She knew that the time had come when she would be forced against her will to undergo the agony, pain and incredible fear that came with electroshock therapy.

The final crash in the manic-depressive cycle is always very devastating for the patient and for everyone involved. I remember that event of March 1952 as if it happened yesterday. The ambulance pulled up in front of the house and when Mother realized what was happening, she took off out the front door and went running down 140th Street as fast as she could wearing nothing but her nightgown.

Kathy and I had become used to chaos in our young lives but this was an emotional event unlike anything I had ever experienced before. The feeling of great sadness for this poor, troubled woman as the ambulance chased her down the street haunts me to this day. It is as if I were out on our front yard in Hawthorne reliving the experience once again. The tears pour down my face as I recall the tragedy of Mother's life. As strange as it may sound, the memory of the events of that night are almost more painful and emotional now than the reality of it was then. And that was more than 50 years ago!

Chapter 7

Electroshock Therapy in the Treatment of Manic-Depressive Illness

Kathy, Mother and Mike
1944

Mike's Chapter

Our experiences with Mother's mental breakdowns started when Kathy and I were toddlers, but the first incident where many of the details are still etched in my mind was Mother's breakdown in 1948. I was eight years old and Kathy was just six. When I look back now, I don't know how we all, especially Dad, survived these events in our lives. As a young child, I couldn't possibly relate to what our father must have been going through.

Our older sister, Patty, stayed with the Champommiere family on this occasion in 1948 and Kathy and I went to a foster home, which I hated. I remember a couple of things vividly about that experience. The man of the house, I assume it was the husband, worked on his car in the garage, until all hours of the night, gunning the engine and keeping everyone awake. The other thing that stands out in my mind was the incident of my confrontation with the mother. She had a son about my age but she was trying to get me to do all the work around the house. One day I got sick of her, her husband, and of being away from Dad. In a heated argument over my household duties, I proceeded to tear all the drapes off the living room windows after which I stormed out the front door. Somehow, I got a hold of Dad and told him that I wanted to come home and that I wasn't going to spend another night with that strange family. I think they were more dysfunctional than we were.

While Dad was dealing with getting his children settled in various homes and continuing to provide for the family, Mother would be going through the extremely frightening ordeal of electroshock therapy.

Upon arrival at the sanitarium, a relatively short ride from our home in Hawthorne, the ambulance attendants would escort

Mother, forcibly if necessary, into a treatment room and start preparing her for the inevitable electroshock therapy. The sight of a pleading patient being dragged into a treatment room and forcibly administered electric currents that cause her jaw to clench, her back to arch, and her body to shake, all while she is being held down by burly attendants was a common one during the 1940s and 1950s but it is not true today. Patients are no longer coerced into treatment. They may be anxious but they enter the treatment room of their own volition. They have been told why the treatment has been recommended and they have given their consent.

According to Dr. Max Fink in his book *Electroshock: Restoring the Mind*, "Electroshock is a treatment for severe and persistent emotional disorders. The physician, following a prescribed procedure, induces an epileptic seizure in the brain. By making sure that the patient's lungs are filled with oxygen, the physician precludes the gasping and difficult breathing that accompany a spontaneous epileptic fit. By relaxing the patient's muscles with chemicals and by inserting a mouth guard, the physician also prevents the tongue biting, fractures and injuries that may occur in epilepsy. The physiologic functions of the body are monitored, and anything out of the ordinary is immediately treated".

Many of these controlled procedures and improvements for the safety and comfort of the patient undergoing the treatment did not come about until the early 1960s and most of Mother's electroshock therapy was administered long before that. When electroshock therapy was introduced, it was administered without anesthetic and patients approached each treatment with anxiety, dread, and panic. Some patients sustained fractures; some died.

I believe that Dad's knowledge of the process was the reason he usually waited as long as possible to have Mother committed. His love for his wife was profound and it was incredibly difficult for him to knowingly subject her to the only treatment he knew of at the time to try to restore her to good health. It's terribly emotional for me to think of what Dad dealt with in this relationship with our mother. I don't think Mother was ever completely well. There were just times that were not as chaotic as others.

I reflect upon reasons why couples today get divorces and I have to shake my head and wonder if some of these couples, with a little more commitment and loyalty to one another, couldn't succeed in having a very meaningful relationship. As husbands and wives age, the more important their history as a couple becomes and often they treasure the commitment they have had to one another. In their own strange way, our parents lived a life of dedication, respect and love for one another.

Electroshock now can be an effective and safe treatment for those with severe mental illness. Yet many patients still consider it so dangerous they fear it as much or more than they fear the disease. The controversy is not about the efficacy of the treatment or its safety, which have been proved, but about the concern that the treatment actually alters the brain, changing a person's personality and character.

One characteristic of bi-polar patients is that in the manic phase they may spend money lavishly and Mother definitely had that problem. Poor Dad. After one of Mother's breakdowns he would always find himself in a serious financial mess. The interesting thing about Mother was that when she was well, she was just the opposite. She never asked for anything for herself. The needs of the family always came first.

We could always tell when Mother was starting into the manic phase of the illness. She became much more talkative and outgoing. It was as though another totally different person was entering and taking over her mind and body. This new person was impatient with everyone and would listen to no one. I remember a particular incident when she got a job at Harris and Frank, an upscale clothing store in Hawthorne. She did quite well until her manic behavior forced management to let her go. I remember her always telling us that she was by far the outstanding salesperson not only in that store, but probably in the entire chain. In the manic stage, the bi-polar person is like an athlete on steroids, believing he or she is invincible, dynamic and unbeatable. Mother was indeed an excellent salesperson and was contributing to the family income until her manic phase kicked in and then her confidence in her skills far exceeded the reality of her commissions. Mother's experience at Harris and Frank took place in 1958 after Patty had been committed to Camarillo State Hospital and was no longer living at home. Up until then, she had had more than enough to keep her busy at home as Patty required her constant care and attention.

In Dr. Max Fink's book, *Electroshock: Restoring the Mind*, he says that "Before electroshock there was no effective treatment for mania. The patient was usually sedated with opiate derivatives, bromides or chloral hydrate. Within a few years of its introduction, electroshock became the main treatment. Then Thorazine and other antipsychotic drugs were used in its place, often in heroic doses to control manic behavior. Later, Lithium, the wonder drug for manic-depressive patients, became the standard treatment. Within the past two decades, anticonvulsant drugs have been prescribed in addition to Lithium or in its stead. Even with this array of medicines some patients remain ill and electroshock becomes the alternative."

I believe that based on the improved methods for administering electroshock therapy, this treatment that was started during the early 1960s, many doctors and experts in the field today might well recommend its use in place of psychotropic drugs such as Lithium. Unfortunately, during the early years of its use, the electroshock treatment was so violent and inhumane that it's never been able to overcome its past and to receive widespread acceptance in the treatment of mental illness.

Chapter 8

The Bond of Motherhood and Only Sons

Mother and Mike

Mike's Chapter

When a child is conceived and nurtured in the womb for a period of time and then comes into this world amidst a mixture of pain and joy, something magical happens. A deep and abiding love is born between Mother and child that we men will never have the privilege to know. Giving birth creates a bond like no other. From the moment of Patty's entry into the world at three pounds until her death 63 years later, Mother was always at her side in mind, body and spirit. These two, mother and daughter, made a connection at Patty's birth and for more than six decades, neither one left the other's thoughts. The relationship of Mother and Patty was the epitome of love and devotion.

One of the things I remember so vividly from when Patty was young was Mother's refusal to cut Patty any slack. She did not baby or pamper Patty just because she happened to be handicapped. Not on your life! Mother expected a lot out of her children and Patty was no exception. Patty wasn't treated any differently than Eileen Thornton's other children. Because of her lack of muscle control, Patty had difficulty holding her head up. When Mother would notice her slumping in her chair, she would let Patty know in no uncertain terms that it was not acceptable behavior.

"Patty, hold your head up straight", could be heard throughout our little house.

I've often marveled, though, at how Mother managed to respond to Patty's every need including helping her at mealtime. While Patty was able to feed herself pretty well, she did require some help with liquids as she had a tendency to choke fairly easily. Mother met all of Patty's needs on a daily basis for the nineteen years she lived at home.

From my earliest years, I never remember Mother as being

The Bond of Motherhood and Only Sons

anything but very different from most people I knew. She was very opinionated and expressed herself with a lot of exuberance. She could be an extremely difficult person at times, in part because of all the issues related to her mental illness. Electroshock therapy, psychotropic drugs and the stigma of being a mentally ill person all contributed to this behavior. Anyone encountering Mother at different times in her life might find her a different person each time they met. Unfortunately, some of her grandkids never knew the Eileen Thornton I knew as a kid. If observers were to view Mother's life strictly in her role as a devoted and dedicated caregiver to her beloved Patty, they may well have regarded her as a saint.

In reflecting on some of my own memories of Mother, a few events jump out at me. One thing that Mother talked about for years was how between the ages of two and four, I called her "Murr". Now, where I got that name I'll never know. Apparently, every time Mother would have her hair done, I would say to her, "Murr's pretty curls". Of course, like a lot of mothers with their sons, Eileen Thornton for pretty much all of her life, thought that everything her son, Michael, said was either cute or brilliant, much to the dismay of the rest of the Thornton family. For many years, Mother told and retold the story of my calling her "Murr", and especially my commenting on Murr's pretty curls.

I have very little memory of my early childhood up to my first day in kindergarten. But for some strange reason, I can recall the memory of entering that schoolhouse as though it were yesterday, when, in fact, it happened more than sixty years ago. Mother and I walked hand-in-hand about four blocks down 140th street to my first experience with formal education, if you want to consider kindergarten as the beginning of formal schooling. In 1946, it actually consisted primarily of painting on large sheets of paper. To this day the entire experience remains incredibly vivid in my mind.

Hawthorne, California, in the 1940s was a somewhat rural area.

She Loved Everyone But Me

There was a lot of open space between the houses and the kids were allowed quite a bit of freedom. I think the parents felt very safe about the comings and goings of their children and so, after the first day of kindergarten, I was on my own going to and coming home from school. When I would get home from school each day, in spite of all the time and attention required to meet Patty's needs, Mother would give me her undivided attention and want to know everything that had happened during my day.

One of my favorite early memories of Mother was her riding horseback English style at Bud's stables in Hawthorne. She looked very impressive sitting on a horse. The stable was only a couple of blocks from our house so we were there quite often. I don't recall where Mother learned to ride, if I ever knew, but she looked the part of an accomplished horsewoman in her riding pants and her tight-fitting high black boots.

Another fond memory of my relationship with Mother was of a college football game she and I went to when I was twelve years old. It was the University of California at Berkeley versus Loyola University. Why Mother and I went to the game, just the two of us, I'm not sure. We had somehow become aware of the All-American fullback at California by the name of Johnny Olszweski and Mother decided that I needed to see him perform. He was an exceptional college football player and he went on to play with the St. Louis Cardinals in the National Football League.

Our family did have a connection with Loyola University since many of the Malloys, my Dad's sister's family, either already attended Loyola or would do so in the future. In fact, in 1957, when I was a Junior and starting quarterback on the Junipero Serra High School football team, we played against my cousin, Tom Malloy, who was a lineman for the Loyola High School team. By the way, we kicked their butts 55-21.

Mother knew that I loved football and this exposure at age 12 to big time college football with the huge crowd and all the

The Bond of Motherhood and Only Sons

excitement was a major catalyst for my interest and later success in football at Serra High School.

It was a day full of thrills for me and one that I have never forgotten. How many mothers take their sons to a major college football game by themselves? She was a special person who did everything she could, including providing regular pep talks about determination and desire, to help me achieve success in sports. One of my biggest disappointments regarding my baseball career with the Los Angeles Dodgers organization is that I never made it to the Major Leagues and wasn't able to give Mother the thrill that she deserved.

There was a period during the fall and winter of 1959 that Mother and I spent a lot of time together. That summer I had played on a Dodger farm club in Kokomo, Indiana, and had returned home to Camarillo, California. After receiving a signing bonus with the Dodgers, I had purchased a small, three-acre lemon grove in Camarillo, a beautiful little town located near the ocean and about one hour north of Los Angeles. My sister, Patty, was a patient at the Camarillo State Hospital and so, once again, we were all together. Dad did an outstanding job tending the lemon grove. The man always had a green thumb when it came to plants or trees. We sold eight crops a year to the Sunkist Lemon Association in Oxnard.

I wasn't working during the baseball off-season and the family at that time was living in a small duplex so Mother and I spent a lot of time together. One of our favorite activities that winter was lunch at the very best Mexican restaurant that I have ever eaten at in my life, El Tecolotte. The owners were from Mexico and did they ever have a great kitchen. None of the waiters spoke English, which gave the place an authentic feel. Mother and I would stuff ourselves with various and assorted Mexican dishes washed down with two or three beers. After some great conversation, we would head back to the house which was only about two miles away. At that point, the stage was set for a terrific afternoon nap. This was our routine at least twice a week. It was a tough winter! I say that facetiously!

Mother talked to me at great length about persistence and never giving up. Kathy also mentions this trait in one of her chapters and it was so true. Mother simply would not allow herself to be overcome by all the obstacles in her life. Some of the decision-making in my life has been less than stellar, but I will never stop trying to reach my potential, to learn from mistakes and to eventually become the man Mother thought I was.

Patty was an angel and she and I had a very special relationship. She viewed me somewhat the way Mother did. I could do no wrong. As Patty matured and her weight climbed to approximately 170 pounds, I was frequently the person who would carry her from the bed to her wheelchair and back again. She was not easy to move due to her handicap and I have often wondered if my ability to carry her about, due to my size, created in her mind something of a special bond between us.

Not everyone is blessed with having a close relationship with a handicapped person and Patty taught me so much about what really matters, what is really important in our lives. During my almost 70 years, whenever I have been down or depressed or feeling sorry for myself, I would think of what Patty had to endure every day of her life and my self-pity would suddenly seem somewhat foolish. Despite her physical limitations, she was almost always bright and cheery and so thankful for any little thing that anyone did for her. Whether it was nurses, doctors, family or friends, many people felt so lucky to know Patty and to be a part of her life. Why do we tend to put so much emphasis on the material things in our lives that are really so unimportant and not nearly enough emphasis on the things that really matter like personal relationships and acts of kindness toward our fellow man?

Mother, Patty and Dad, what an amazing trio! They were one

in mind, body and spirit. Their lives were devoted to one another in their own special way and this book is a tribute to them. Their individual sacrifices for one another did not go unnoticed and, despite what might not have been properly conveyed during their lifetimes, we are now expressing our incredible admiration for their devotion to one another. We hope that what they endured in support of each other and the deep and abiding love they had for one another will set an example and provide a standard for our family and all families for years to come.

She Loved Everyone But Me

Mike and Patty, Mike's 1st Birthday, April 14, 1941

Chapter 9

My Dad and I—A Complicated Relationship

Mike and Dad
June 9, 1989

Mike's Chapter

I can picture Dad in my mind, with such grace and athleticism, running down 140th Street. I would hit him on the dead run and he would make an over-the-shoulder catch of the football. He was definitely the most athletic and most fun Dad in our entire working-class neighborhood. In the early 1950s Hawthorne, California was still a somewhat rural little town in the Los Angeles area about three miles inland from Manhattan Beach. Our home at 5008 W. 140th Street was purchased by our folks in 1944 for the huge sum of $3,000 and it would be our family home for the next 15 years. It was situated on a good-sized lot and we had a beautiful yard. Mother and Dad both had green thumbs and all during their married life, Dad's yards were typically the show place of the neighborhood. I remember that frequently cars would stop in front of our house and admire the landscaping before they moved on. Mother had a greenhouse that was full of beautiful begonias and ferns and with my help, Dad always saw that our yard was well kept. We had chickens and rabbits and cats and dogs and a big eucalyptus tree to climb in. It was a fun house and a fun neighborhood most of the time.

Dad was a great athlete and all around student at Cathedral High School in Los Angeles. Entries in the Cathedral yearbook gave evidence that he was looked up to as a class leader and captain of the football team. He was also vice president of the student body. In a picture of the Cathedral varsity football team hanging on the wall in my dining room Dad looks very handsome and rugged in his stance at right end. This young man, Robert J. Thornton, appeared to be headed for big things and what would seem to be a very bright future. It was not for him to know then that the events over the next ten years would shape his future and define the

My Dad and I—A Complicated Relationship

possibilities for the remaining 60 years of his life. His future wife, our mother, Eileen, would have her first of many nervous breakdowns in 1931 and would be diagnosed as having manic-depressive illness.

Dad was a traveling salesman for a flooring company when he and Mother married. I'm not sure why he didn't continue his education and graduate from college. His father was a successful businessman and I don't believe money was the issue. After he married and started a family, Dad left the traveling job and went to work at a Texaco gas station for $30 per month. Eventually, he moved on to work at Cohen's stone yard in Inglewood. In a short period of time, he became a self employed stonemason, a skill and profession that he pursued for most of his working life.

My most vivid memories of Dad and our relationship begin when I was 10 years old. I was beginning to play Little League baseball and Dad was always very supportive of me and willing to work with me in improving my skills. He was about six feet tall and weighed about 180 lbs. Well into his 50s and even in his early 60s, he could walk on his hands and do a standing flip off the ground. The hard work as a stonemason kept him in good shape and he thoroughly enjoyed throwing the ball around with me whether it be a baseball or a football.

Starting in Little League, I excelled at sports and Mom and Dad were always very supportive, going to all my games from that time right on through high school and beyond. When I began my professional baseball career, they followed it very closely and with much enthusiasm.

When I was about age 13, I started helping Dad during the summer as a laborer, mixing concrete and hauling the stone around from the truck to the job site. I met many of the people who were part of Dad's working life, including other masons and bricklayers, and the owner of the stone yard where he purchased his different types of stone and rock as well as all the associated materials such as sand and cement.

Other people in Dad's life were bartenders scattered around the greater Los Angeles area with whom he would occasionally visit at lunch time or when he dropped in for a quick beer after work. Drinking a beer for lunch wouldn't slow Dad down one bit. He was an incredibly hard worker. Even during the most chaotic of times in his life, when Mother was having a nervous breakdown that resulted in a trip to a sanitarium, Dad never missed a day's work and he kept our family together. He dealt with all the challenges involved in raising three, and eventually four young children and maintained stability in our lives.

Dad had an excellent reputation in the southern California area as a master craftsman and frequently we worked on fireplaces and slate floors for some of the wealthier people in the area. Bob Thornton was loved by all who knew him, the people he worked for, other men he knew in all the different trades, or bartenders that he saw on a fairly frequent basis. Dad was an extremely likable fellow. Everyone greeted him by name and they always seemed happy to see him.

Wherever we went, Dad would proudly introduce me as his son. I remember how good that made me feel and that's something I'll never forget. I think I was about 14 years old when one day after work we went into a bar in Inglewood that I had never been in and Dad introduced me to the bartender and owner of the establishment. He was the largest man that I had ever seen in my young life and I recall that he had the strangest looking ears. I don't remember his name (it's been 50 years) but Dad pointed out to me that he had been the heavyweight wrestling Champion of the world and that his funny-looking ears were called "cauliflower ears". Many men who have wrestled for any length of time eventually have this condition. Apparently the holding of your opponent in a headlock, a popular wrestling maneuver, by these men with big powerful arms, leads to this form of disfigurement. In glancing

My Dad and I—A Complicated Relationship

around the bar I noticed pictures of his wrestling career and I also remembered that this huge man was very soft spoken and polite in contrast to his terribly frightening appearance. Some 55 years later, I remember this as having been a really neat day with my Dad.

My relationship with my father was fairly complex. It had its good side but at times was very unpleasant. I think part of the problem started at my birth. Mother had been dealing with Patty for approximately 18 months when along came this extremely healthy baby boy who immediately became the apple of her eye. Mother loved Patty dearly and devoted a great portion of her life to taking care of this little girl with cerebral palsy but a healthy boy who turned out to be an exceptionally good athlete was something that Mother was never able to deal with objectively. Until her death at the ripe old age of 86, she felt that I could do no wrong and when Dad would criticize or attempt to discipline me, Mother would rush to my defense. My parents had many arguments about my behavior and about me in general. Dad was very critical, especially when he was drinking, and Mother probably was too much to the other extreme.

Robert J. Thornton, our Dad, was one of the nicest, most polite and mild mannered people you could ever meet-when he was sober. What a great smile he had! It made you feel good all over. Unfortunately, Dad had a problem with alcohol. I'm sure that dealing with Mother's manic-depressive illness, Patty's handicap and all the financial hardships resulting from these situations made him want to escape at times to some other happier and less stressful world.

When he was drinking, Dad was a nightmare and he drank frequently. After four or five beers and a shot of whiskey, he would rant and rave about his favorite subject, politics. Dad was the liberal Rush Limbaugh. As far as he was concerned, the Republicans were out to eliminate or break the working man and the unions that protected him. Being a proud Irishman, his other

She Loved Everyone But Me

favorite subject was the struggle between the Irish and the English. He couldn't discuss this subject with any kind of control or objectivity. One might have thought that he had been a farmer in Ireland during the potato famine instead of a child who had left the Emerald Isle behind when he was three years old.

One thing I remember clearly in regards to Dad's behavior, whether he was sober or inebriated, is that in all the years our family of six lived together in the rather cramped quarters of that little house on 140th Street, and with all the chaos and tragedy that occurred at times, I never once ever heard Dad raise his voice or be cruel to or critical of Patty. He was sweet and kind to her at all times and she loved him dearly and he loved her.

Dad was a huge boxing fan. We always watched the Wednesday and Friday night fights on television and I was given my first set of boxing gloves when I was ten or eleven. I was frequently the victim of Dad's boxing skills when he would arrive home after a few too many drinks. Although he never injured me, between the ages of twelve and fifteen, I was frightened of Dad. Home was not a fun place to be when he arrived there inebriated.

Kathy was tougher than I was. She would go toe to toe with Dad and attempt to settle him down. She usually had some success and was able to convince him that eating dinner and going to bed might be the best thing to do, especially since he would have to get up early and work hard all the next day. By age 16, I had grown to 6ft 3in and weighed 180 lbs. Dad was no longer able to intimidate me and he never really tried. I can't even imagine how difficult these situations must have been for Mother; in a 1,200-sq. ft. house. Most everything that is said by anyone can be heard by everyone else there.

Human behavior is a mystery. After living through these experiences involving alcohol abuse as a youngster, I might predictably have grown up to be a teetotaler . Instead, between the ages of 25 and 40, I also abused alcohol in various ways. I lost jobs,

My Dad and I—A Complicated Relationship

experienced difficulties at home, poured money down the drain. I am so thankful that my son, Michael, has broken the string of problem drinkers in the Thornton family. He is a perfect gentleman at all times. He never rants and raves if someone disagrees with him and he doesn't abuse alcohol. He is a social drinker and I don't think I've ever seen him intoxicated. Thank God, he and I have never had a major confrontation.

This subject of my father's alcohol abuse is difficult to acknowledge and to write about. Dad had so many good qualities that we all admired but, unfortunately, we did not express that admiration to him while he was alive. Most of the time, Dad and I got along fine and my overall memories of our relationship are very positive. I miss him and grieve over him to this day and he's been gone for 19 years. The inability of many men to express their love and affection for one another, even among family members, creates emotional difficulty when the time comes for final separation. I don't seem to miss Mother and Patty as much as I do Dad and I think it's because my relationship with them was so much more open. We didn't hide our feeling for one another. I was crazy about them and they felt the same way about me. They were definitely two of my biggest boosters. When I say I don't miss them as much as I do Dad, it's not that the loss is not as great; it's just that with Dad there are so many things that were left unsaid. I would give everything I have in life in the way of material possessions to have one more day with him. It's much easier to accept a loved one's passing when all the feelings between you have been expressed and love has not gone unexpressed.

In attempting to address this subject of Dad's behavior when he drank excessively, I think there's a lot more to say than that he was a poor drinker and so became difficult to deal with. As a standout during his high school years at Cathedral, as captain of the football team and as a class leader, Dad was also an exceptionally handsome young man. I'm sure he was confident that he had a bright future.

His own Father was a successful businessman but he died at a young age and wasn't able to give his son some of the benefits of his success. Dad's sisters, Louise and Marjorie, married men who did quite well financially. Bud owned a large mortuary in Los Angeles and Emmett had a storm drain construction company that produced a great deal of wealth for Louise and their nine children. Mother had a brother, Frank, who was a very successful attorney. To top it off Dad's older brother, Gerald, would become vice-president of one of the largest airlines in the world at that time, TWA.

While other family members were achieving this extremely high level of success, Dad was struggling to take care of a wife who was mentally ill, his oldest daughter, Patty, who was born with cerebral palsy, and a growing young family. Patty required a tremendous amount of care and this certainly made Mother's attempts to stabilize her life more difficult. During his thirties and forties Dad's focus was not on a career or building a future or on creating security for his family. It was all about dealing with the next crisis as it occurred. When would Eileen, his wife, have another breakdown and have to be placed in a sanitarium and how would he manage working and taking care of his four young children by himself? Dad never showed any resentment about the unfortunate circumstances that he had to deal with on a somewhat regular basis. I don't recall his ever making a critical comment to Mother about how her breakdowns over the years had in any way hampered his ability to achieve a significant level of success.

Dad was quite remarkable in the way he always supported Mother. There's no question that Eileen and Patty were a great source of mental strain on our father as their issues presented very difficult challenges. Part of that strain was the tremendous effort both Dad and Mom made for many years trying to enable Patty to get out of her wheelchair and walk like the rest of us. Their efforts were truly heroic.

My Dad and I—A Complicated Relationship

Financially, Dad was never able to get his head above water; between Patty's leg braces, wheelchairs and multiple surgeries and Mother's periodic nervous breakdowns, he was never able to build any kind of financial stability. I believe these circumstances in his life took a considerable toll on him but he never expressed any bitterness to anyone. In many respects, Dad was a very strong man who showed tremendous character under pressure. Anyone who was around him when he was having a particularly bad drinking episode could detect the long-repressed anger that would suddenly be manifested. At these times and only at these times would his pent-up frustrations and anger over his plight in life come out.

At a young age, I didn't have the wisdom to understand all this and only saw the rather ugly results of excessive alcohol consumption. Despite some of the unpleasant circumstances surrounding Dad's drinking and knowing what he had to endure throughout his life, I will go to my grave feeling tremendous respect and love for him. I only hope that the teachings of Catholicism are correct and that we will be united someday and I will have the opportunity to express belatedly my understanding and appreciation for who he was as a complete person and my respect for what he did for us as a family.

In June of 1958, I graduated from Junipero Serra High School, an all boys Catholic school located in Gardena, California. This south central L.A. community was wide open in the 1950s. There were gambling casinos, burlesque shows and many other activities that fascinated 18-year-old boys. The night of my graduation from high school I went home after the ceremony to change clothes in preparation for attending one of the many parties that would be taking place that evening.

Upon arriving at the house, I noticed a strange car in the driveway. Much to my surprise, two scouts for the Los Angeles Dodgers were in our living room talking to the folks. Jackie Warner and Lefty Phillips were there to attempt to sign me to a professional baseball contract. I had been a fairly dominant pitcher for the past three years in the Catholic League but I had no idea that there were any major league teams taking a serious look at me. I was going to college to play football on a scholarship and baseball was the furthest thing from my mind. Those gentleman were good salesman. By noon the next day I was in downtown Los Angeles signing a bonus contract with the Dodgers. They had just that year moved the franchise from Brooklyn, where they had been for many years, to Los Angeles. Mother and Dad were both very proud and it was an exciting time for all of us. We used some of my bonus money to purchase a three-acre lemon grove in Camarillo. In 1959, Camarillo was a beautiful little town of 4,000 people located 60 miles north of Los Angeles and about an hour's drive south of Santa Barbara. This picturesque area was mainly agricultural, primarily lemons, oranges and avocados. We joined the Sunkist Lemon Association and they harvested eight pickings a year. Dad tended the grove while I was playing ball and for two or three years, I think he was the happiest I had ever seen him. The man should have been a farmer. He definitely had a green thumb and did he ever enjoy taking exceptionally good care of those lemons.

It was a great feeling of satisfaction for me that by having the resources to purchase this property, I was able to help Dad enjoy some of the best years of his life. Unfortunately, the lemons did not produce enough income to sustain Mom and Dad indefinitely and Dad went to work driving a Helms Bakery truck. It was another one of the many transitions he had made in his life but we would never hear him complain or show any sign of disappointment. Typical of everything he did in his life, he approached this new job with professionalism and a willingness to work hard. The man was a perfectionist. Why is it so hard to truly appreciate the people in our lives while they are with us?

I have very limited memories of my earliest years. Surprisingly, I do have extremely vivid recollections of one of Kathy's and my

My Dad and I—A Complicated Relationship

experiences in a foster home. I was four years old and the lady we stayed with, Mrs. Defrier, was very sweet and kind. My sister and I were fond of her. Kathy had just turned three and I believe this was our second stay at Mrs. Defrier's home and as foster homes go, we were fairly comfortable and content.

At the same time I remember being sad and lonely. Every evening about 5:00, I would walk out to the end of the driveway and wait for Dad, hoping he would be coming to pick Kathy and me up and take us home. It's amazing to me that to this day, some 65 years later, I can remember that time in my life as if it were yesterday. I don't recall much of anything else going back that far. I do remember Mrs. Defrier living in downtown Los Angeles and I don't think that on this occasion, we were with her for any longer than three months. I can still remember the Defrier house in great detail and whenever my mind wanders back to that time in my life, the feelings and emotions I felt come rising up and the pain and loneliness is with me all over again. Most evenings after standing on the curb for about thirty minutes, I would tearfully wander back into the house, knowing that Dad wasn't coming and that Mother must still be in the sanitarium and not well enough for us to go home. I often wonder why this time is like a permanent snapshot in my mind that never fades away. In a way, Dad was my hero during this time. He was the only one who could return me to the safety of our home.

In January of 1966, Bob and Eileen Thornton started on a new and exciting phase of their life. They got in the car and headed for Idaho. Kathy had lived in Twin Falls with her husband, Bill Crow, for about five years. Bill was born and raised in Twin Falls, a farming community in south central Idaho with a population of about 25,000. It was close to world-class fishing and over the next 20 years, they enjoyed many wonderful days on the banks of Idaho's most beautiful streams and creeks, trying to hook the ever elusive rainbow trout. Dad could take his rod and reel and a cooler of cold beer and sandwiches, and head for the Hagerman Valley, mainly Riley Creek, to spend the entire day trying to hook and land as many fish as possible. For him, it was still a great day in Paradise even if he came home empty-handed. Fishing was a recreational activity that Dad had enjoyed most of his life. Some of my fondest memories as a youngster between the ages of seven and fourteen were when Dad and I would go fishing for halibut on the piers at either Manhattan Beach or Redondo Beach. For some reason we usually went at night, I guess that was when the fish were biting, leaving the house in Hawthorne at about 7:00 in the evening and getting home at about eleven. Hawthorne was only about four miles from the ocean, so it was convenient to go fishing often.

Fishing for trout in Idaho was a totally different experience than fishing in the ocean and required much more patience and skill. Dad was an exceptionally good fisherman, probably because he had a world of patience. He became very skillful at hooking these beautiful fish. Life in Idaho was good. The change was having a very therapeutic effect on Mother and Dad, but true to form during the 30 years of their marriage, the roof was about to fall in.

Mother's final breakdown occurred in 1969, but unlike many of the previous episodes she had experienced in her life, this one ended on a positive note. Dr. Briggs, a psychiatrist in Twin Falls, introduced Mother to what at the time was an experimental drug that turned out to be the miracle drug for those suffering from manic-depressive illness. It was Lithium. Mother was stable for the next thirty years of her life.

In about 1980, Dad and I had probably the most dramatic and painful confrontation of our lives and didn't speak to one another for approximately three years. We had both been drinking too much at their mobile home outside of Twin Falls and there was an exchange of cruel statements, topped off by my telling him that he didn't have the decency to go to his own sister Marjorie's funeral in Los Angeles. She had died within the past year or two. The folks

My Dad and I—A Complicated Relationship

were on a tight budget at that time and I'm sure that's why they didn't make the trip to Los Angeles. Dad was not only hurt but he was furious and I not only have to regret my statement but I have to live with it for the rest of my life. With the help and persistence of my wife, Sheryl, we finally made our peace and these two crazy Irishmen went back to being father and son and affectionate in our own way with one another until Dad's death in October of 1990. Every family needs a peacekeeper and that has always been Sheryl's role in our family. I thank God for her in so many different ways.

Dad had a heart attack in 1987 and lost 40 percent of his heart muscle. He was taken to the Twin Falls Clinic, and after one or two days, the decision was made to take him by ambulance to St. Luke's Hospital in Boise, a facility that had one of the finest cardiac care units in the country. Our father was not doing well and the doctors decided that even though the 2-hour trip from Twin Falls to Boise was risky, it was necessary. Following the ambulance in our car for 135 miles was a frightening and stressful experience, not knowing if Dad would survive the trip. Fortunately, his condition was stabilized and he had three more reasonably good years.

In early September of 2005, almost 15 years after Dad's death, I was watching one of the ESPN sports channels that gives the life history of some of the greatest athletes of the 20th century. This particular show featured the life and times of the great Irish fighter, Billy Conn, and in particular his much heralded fight against Joe Louis for the Heavyweight Championship of the World in 1941. Louis, who was arguably the greatest heavyweight boxer of all time, was an imposing 204 lbs and had a reliable knockout punch. The scrappy Conn was a skilled boxer who had held the Middleweight and Light Heavyweight crowns and was confident that despite weighing only 169 lbs, he could whip the much larger Louis. After months of hype, the fight was held at Madison Square Garden in New York City, the site of many of the great boxing matches of our time. ESPN showed every minute of every round and after hearing

Dad talk about this great fight as a kid, I was actually seeing this battle for the first time. I was only a year old when the fight actually took place, but I wonder if Dad had me sitting by the radio with him in 1941.

I was alone in the family room the night I actually saw the fight and after the first three or four rounds, Dad was there with me. We were watching Conn outbox the much larger Louis for the first 12 rounds of a 15-round fight. The crowd at the Garden was going crazy. They were watching what would be the biggest upset in boxing history. Billy Conn was a handsome and maybe too confident and cocky Irishman. Dad thought he was the greatest. Conn's overconfidence turned out to be his undoing and instead of staying away from Louis and protecting his lead, he told his corner between the 12th and 13th rounds that he was going to knock Louis out. The rest is history. In Round 13, Louis caught Conn with a vicious left hook and being the great finisher that he was, knocked Billy Conn out. Dad told me the story of this great and colorful Irish boxer many times and it was exciting to finally see this fight together.

In her autobiography, Jane Pauley, the former host of the Today show, said that her father spent his life "mourning the person he thought he was". Our Dad, Robert Thornton, sacrificed who he might have been because of his loyalty and love for two amazing women who needed him, our mother and our sister. He was a great man and I loved and respected him very much.

Chapter 10

Welcome Travelers

Patty and Mother
1942

Kathy's Chapter

"Welcome Travelers" was Mother and Patty's favorite television program during the 1950s. They would watch it faithfully together each day, Mother on the sofa with her tea and cigarettes, Patty in her wheelchair with her eyes glued to our little 15-inch Philco. The personal stories with which "travelers" to the show regaled the audience carried Mother and Patty into another world where they were totally caught up in the trials and tribulations of these new friends. Because these guests were real people with real triumphs and tragedies, their stories hit home with Mother and Patty to a much greater degree than the soap operas of the day.

I remember so clearly coming home from elementary school and receiving a detailed report on the "travelers" who had been welcomed to that day's program. Almost from the beginning of their addiction to "Welcome Travelers", Patty began urging Mother to write and tell "their story". This was in response to a message at the end of each program that encouraged the viewers to send in their stories. The viewers whose stories were chosen would be flown, all expenses paid, to Chicago, be put up in a luxury hotel and appear on the program. Each traveler also was given an extravagant array of gifts.

Patty figured, "Why not us?" After months of relentless daily nagging, Patty finally wore down Mother's resistance and they began writing. Before long, they had "their story" in the mail. Then began the daily vigil of waiting by the mailbox for a response from the program. The two of them had just about given up hope of ever being chosen when lo and behold —a large envelope arrived with a letter informing Mother that "Welcome Travelers" was most definitely interested in having her come to Chicago and tell their viewers about herself and Patty. Talk about excitement! The two of

Welcome Travelers

them were so thrilled.

Dad took Mom shopping for some new outfits for her trip (a rare occurrence in itself) and before we knew it, we were waving her off on the train. Never one to be shy, she knew the life story of almost every passenger in her car by the time the train reached Chicago. She particularly enjoyed the company of a group of young sailors who were headed home for the holidays.

Once in the "Windy City", Mom literally had the time of her life. Just escaping the responsibilities of home and family for the first time since her marriage was a tremendous treat for her. Put on top of that a three-day stay in a luxury hotel, dining in gourmet restaurants, being catered to like a television star and Mom felt as if she'd died and gone to heaven. Her trip home was by plane, another first for her, and she received a hearty welcome from a family who had dearly missed her.

For months, the family and all our friends were regaled with stories of Mom's trip and her most attentive listener was Patty. The whole experience was a triumph for this mother and daughter who had been through so many struggles together. They were ecstatic that they had pulled it off and would delight in recalling the memories of every little detail for years to come.

Patty had originally hoped that they would share this adventure but when the invitation came, it was for Mother only. Patty never uttered a word of complaint, however, and thoroughly enjoyed the experience vicariously. The day the program aired, we all stayed home from school and sat glued to the television. We proudly watched as Mother told her story. Patty always felt that this trip was a special gift she had given to Mother because if it hadn't been for her persistence in pushing Mother to write to "Welcome Travelers", she never would have had this unforgettable experience. Patty saw it as a great way to thank Mother for all she had done for her. The joy they shared in this achievement further strengthened the bonds of their special relationship.

She Loved Everyone But Me

Before the excitement even began to die down, a huge delivery truck arrived in front of our home and began to disgorge a steady stream of Mother's "Welcome Travelers" prizes. Many were the open mouths and wide eyes on 140th St. that day as one after another the deliverymen carried into our home: a refrigerator (no more ice box for us), stove, circular sofa, round maple coffee table, two lighted landscape paintings and the piece de resistance, as far as we kids were concerned, a huge maple console television set! We all felt so fancy with these beautiful new furnishings brightening up our little home, not to mention how much Mother, an outstanding cook, enjoyed the luxury of her sparkling new kitchen appliances. Cloud Nine was covered with Thorntons that day!

The remarkable story that Mother told on "Welcome Travelers" was a story the likes of which have touched the hearts of humans since the beginning of time, a story of love, devotion, self-sacrifice, mutual support, perseverance and companionship. Mother and Patty were as close emotionally as any mother and daughter could be. Their lives were completely intertwined. When Patty came home from the hospital after spending the first three months of her life in an incubator, she did not develop normally. By the time she had been diagnosed with cerebral palsy, our brother, Michael John, had been born and I was on the way. Many of my earliest childhood memories are of visits to the Crippled Children's Hospital in downtown Los Angeles where Patty, under the supervision of her favorite physician, Dr. Von Brisen, was receiving treatments and undergoing surgeries. These trips to the hospital were all-day affairs. Mother did not drive and Dad had to work every day to keep our family's ship afloat so we would take three buses and a streetcar to transport ourselves to the hospital. Patty could not walk so Mother would carry her in her arms. Mike and I were instructed to hang on tightly to Mother's skirt as she shepherded us through this transportation system. Having since had three children in stair-step fashion myself, I marvel at how

Mother managed this amazing feat. My daughters were all healthy and I had a car to transport us and still, at times, I was at wit's end. Memories of how my own mother rose above so many challenges to get Patty the treatment she needed leave me in awe. I can't imagine doing even once what my mother did on a regular basis. As Chapin so profoundly put it: "No language can express the power and beauty and heroism of a mother's love."

Mother was obsessed with trying to make Patty "normal" and able to function like other children. Much of her day was spent working with Patty; exercising her limbs according to the instructions of the physical therapists, putting on and periodically adjusting her leg braces, standing her up in her custom made table which was created by our dear family friend, Jean Barry. The purpose of this table was to strengthen Patty's legs and accustom them to bearing her weight. And, of course, Mother daily took care of Patty's grooming and hygiene needs, bathing, dressing, toileting, etc. Caring for Patty was almost a full-time job for Mother and yet she always seemed to have time for each of her children.

Mother often mentioned how grateful she was that Patty was able to talk and communicate with the family, an ability that not all victims of cerebral palsy share. This was a blessing for us all and Patty was never shy about contributing her opinions to family discussions. She also could feed herself and had limited use of her hands with their double-jointed fingers.

Mother was determined that Patty should receive an education. She alternated between attending schools for the handicapped and being home-schooled by teachers provided by the state of California. Throughout Patty's grade school days, Mother never lost hope that her daughter would one day walk. There were surgeries to Patty's knees and ankles to lessen the spasticity and finally an exploratory brain surgery to see if something could be done neurologically to help her. None of these surgeries proved beneficial, much to Mother's disappointment. In spite of her limitations, Patty seemed to thoroughly enjoy her childhood.

Although we had to cope with Patty's handicaps, Mother's bouts with mental illness, and Dad's drinking problems, we Thornton's, for the most part, enjoyed a happy home in which our over-riding love for one another seemed to mitigate the negative aspects of life. The two family members who exemplified this loving and devoted relationship the most were Mother and Patty. It was their story that Mother told in a self-effacing way on "Welcome Travelers".

She Loved Everyone But Me

Mother's guiding hand, faithfuly striving to steer Patty safely throught life, 1943

Chapter 11

Life Just Isn't Fair

Patty and Kathy
1946

Kathy's Chapter

Patty was my "big sis". She was an important part of my life from the very beginning. She was born in 1938, I in 1941. Until her death in 2002 I didn't know what life was like without her. All my life I loved her, cared for her and shared a closeness that was unique to my relationship with her.

Over the years whenever I heard people whiningly make the statement, "Life just isn't fair," I'd think to myself, "You're darn right it isn't." This truth is graphically illustrated every day for those with a handicapped sibling. My legs worked fine, Patty's didn't. I could bathe and dress and go to the bathroom by myself, she couldn't. I could run all over the neighborhood playing baseball, kick-the-can and football, she couldn't.

I learned early, deep in my heart-of-hearts, that life is most definitely not fair. Whenever one of us kids would complain to Mother about something Patty said or did, her response was, "Just remember, young lady, there but for the grace of God go you!"

Not that our family members were obsessed with feeling sorry for Patty. Quite the contrary was true. Mother's obsession was trying with all her being to make Patty's life as normal as possible and the rest of us were expected to help her reach that goal. She insisted that Patty be involved in all of our daily activities. Patty had a large tray fitted to her wheelchair and that became her work and play center. If we were doing laundry, Patty folded clothes. If we were washing dishes, she dried the silverware. If we were baking, she stirred the batter. She was always an integral part of our daily lives and activities.

At play, Patty held one end of the jump rope while I held the other end. Together we turned it as our friends jumped. She loved board games such as checkers, Monopoly and Chinese checkers. Whatever the game, Patty played it with a deep desire to win. We

Life Just Isn't Fair

Thornton's were a very competitive bunch. Second place never appealed very much to any of us, including Patty.

Patty loved to read and took great pride in her ability to read. She and I would take turns reading out loud to each other for hours on end. *Anne of Green Gables* was a particular childhood favorite of hers.

In 1947 Patty was chosen to be the Easter Seal poster child, an experience that vividly lived on in her memories throughout the rest of her life. Talking about it always brought a smile to her face as she launched into a lengthy reminiscence about traveling to Warner Brothers Studios to meet, have her picture taken and eat lunch in the studio commissary with Barry Fitzgerald and Wanda Hendrix, two prominent film stars of the 1940s. She was presented with a hat that was completely covered in Easter Seals, which she treasured as a fond memento of an unforgettable honor and experience.

Needless to say, the Thornton family became great supporters of the Easter Seal Society, not financially, as that was impossible given our ongoing struggles to make ends meet, but most definitely as volunteers. I can't begin to count all the donation envelopes we stuffed as kids. Big boxes of them would arrive at our door each spring and we spent many an evening preparing them for mailing.

A prominent women's sorority in the Los Angeles area became aware of Patty as a result of her being chosen the Easter Seal Society poster child. They decided to make her the recipient of their annual project to brighten the life of a child in their community. That is how Neva came into our lives.

Neva was the most beautiful porcelain doll ever created. She had black curly hair like Patty's and was about the size of the eighteen-inch American Girl dolls that are so popular today. Neva came complete with her own trunk filled with a wardrobe that would have made Grace Kelly proud. She also brought along a white satin-covered book with her name stitched on it and her life story inside.

She Loved Everyone But Me

Patty and I felt as if we'd hit the jackpot! We spent countless hours playing with this incredible doll, dressing her in all her gorgeous gowns and furs and allowing our imaginations to run wild creating all kinds of adventures for her. We thought we were the luckiest girls in the world! Nowadays, American Girl type dolls with fancy wardrobes are much more common. All four of my granddaughters, as well as most of their friends, have one but in the 1940s when we were kids, Patty was the only girl we knew who owned such a splendid toy.

The Crippled Children's Hospital in Los Angeles, where Patty received much of her medical care, held an annual Christmas party, an eagerly anticipated event by all of us Thornton kids. One party that is etched in my memory featured Roy Rogers and his horse, Trigger. We had all seen Roy and Trigger in the movies but to see them in person was a real thrill. Trigger was amazing, doing all kinds of tricks at Roy's command, including counting with his hoof. We were enthralled! Santa Claus checked in from the North Pole and each child at the party received a gift, items we soon forgot, but we never forgot Roy and Trigger. For months afterward, Patty and I fantasized about having all kinds of wonderful adventures with those two memorable movie stars.

What was education like for handicapped children in Southern California in the 1940s? Patty alternated between attending a school especially for the handicapped, Harlan Schumaker in Inglewood, and being home-schooled by two exceptional special education teachers, Mrs. Halverson and Mrs. Kanoff. When Patty attended Harlan Schumaker, a bus picked her up at our door each morning and delivered her home each afternoon, a real blessing for our non-driving mother. A special memory I have of Harlan Schumaker was a spaghetti dinner our family attended there. The spaghetti couldn't hold a candle to Mom's but they had a lot of games and activities for the kids so, as the saying goes, "A great time was had by all."

Between the school and the home teachers, Patty learned to

read and print. Her double-jointed and palsied hands would never allow her to write in cursive. The proudest moment of her formal education came in 1979 when she received her G.E.D. in Pocatello, Idaho.

Patty's favorite vacation memory was a week-long trip to Camp Paivika, a summer camp for handicapped children in the San Bernardino National Forest. The camp was founded in 1947 and was equipped to provide kids like Patty with the opportunity to participate in traditional camping activities such as swimming, horseback riding, hiking and crafts. Patty did it all and loved every minute of it but her favorite activity was singing around the campfire. She brought home a book of camp songs, which she taught me, and the two of us sang them together for years afterward. I can still remember the words of the Camp Paivika song: "Over hill, over dale we will hit the dusty trail as Paivikans go marching along."

When Patty, Mike and I were all in our teens, it became extremely stressful for Patty to see Mike and me enjoying all the exciting activities of high school life. We were constantly on the go with school, dates, dances, football games, etc. When we were younger, it was easy to include Patty in our games and activities but as we all entered our teens, it became more difficult. Patty would often tell us how she would love to join us in all our teenage pursuits. She had the normal desires of a teenager and wanted a boyfriend just as I did but by the time I was a freshman at Marymount High, her life was pretty much confined to our home. Now, once again, the confluence of nature and nurture entered into the lives of the Thornton family.

Patty may have been born with a pre-disposition to mental illness but the question is: Are people with such pre-dispositions more sensitive to negative events in life? Did the frustration of seeing Mike and me engaging in activities that were beyond her reach trigger her mental illness or would she have succumbed to this condition no matter what?

She Loved Everyone But Me

Whatever the cause, Patty's behavior became increasingly erratic. She began refusing to eat and lost a lot of weight. In 1957, at the age of 18, she had her first mental breakdown, which was characterized by hallucinations and non-stop talking. With the help of our family doctor, Mother nursed her through the breakdown, hoping it was just an isolated incident. When the hallucinations, non-stop talking and refusing to eat started up again in 1958, at the suggestion of the family doctor, Mike drove Mother and Patty to the General Hospital in Los Angeles. The psychiatrists there did a three-day evaluation, diagnosed Patty's illness as a chronic condition and recommended that she be transferred to the Camarillo State Hospital for the mentally ill in Camarillo, California.

Mother could hardly believe her ears. Throughout Patty's life she had tried to make things as normal as possible for her and now this! A few years earlier Mother had finally faced the reality that Patty would never walk and she had begun looking into vocational training for her. At one point, she contacted an order of nuns in Arizona who accepted handicapped candidates but discovered to hers and Patty's disappointment that Patty's disabilities were too severe for her to be considered at that convent. And now that Patty had reached the age of nineteen years came this diagnosis of severe and chronic mental illness. To all of us in the family it seemed like an incredible case of piling on!

After discussing the matter extensively, Mom and Dad decided to give the hospital a try and thus began the most difficult nine years of Patty's life. Living in a mental hospital in the 1950s was a little taste of hell on earth. Effective psychotropic drugs were still a decade away and so Patty's environment in the institution was one of constant noise and bizarre behavior. Mom and Dad, most often accompanied by Colleen and me, would make the 120-mile round-trip to Camarillo each weekend to give Patty a break and get her out for picnics and other family activities. Finally, after I graduated from Marymount High School in June of 1959, our family made a permanent move to Camarillo to be closer to Patty.

Thus it was that when Mother had her nervous breakdown in Camarillo in 1960 and was hospitalized at the Camarillo State Hospital, Patty had already been living there for two years.

Having a handicapped sister in one's life affords an opportunity for a relationship unlike any other. From the time I was a small child, the love and gratitude I received from Patty over the years was always so heart-warming to me. Unhampered by the demands of a schedule most of us must adhere to in our lives, she always had time for me. Whatever I wanted to do sounded exciting to her. Even as she got older and her mental illness sometimes provoked her into unkindness, she was always very apologetic to me later and genuinely broken-hearted about causing me pain.

When my husband, Bill, was suffering from life-threatening metastatic lung cancer in 2001, Patty was so supportive of me. She called frequently from her home at the Main Street House in Jerome expressing her concern for how Bill's chemotherapy treatment was going and reminding me that she was praying for him daily. She was totally understanding about our not being able to get together for our weekly visits and outings together, as we had always done. Her concern was for me and Bill and how we were holding up through this frightening ordeal. One evening, when we were talking on the phone, Patty brought me to tears when she said, "Kathy, I'm really worried about you. You and Bill have been married for so long. I don't know if you'll be able to go on if anything happens to him." Her heartfelt concern really touched me. When Bill went into remission six months later, Patty was certain it was her prayers that had saved him and I thanked her profusely. She was a real pal and I miss her terribly now that she is gone.

She Loved Everyone But Me

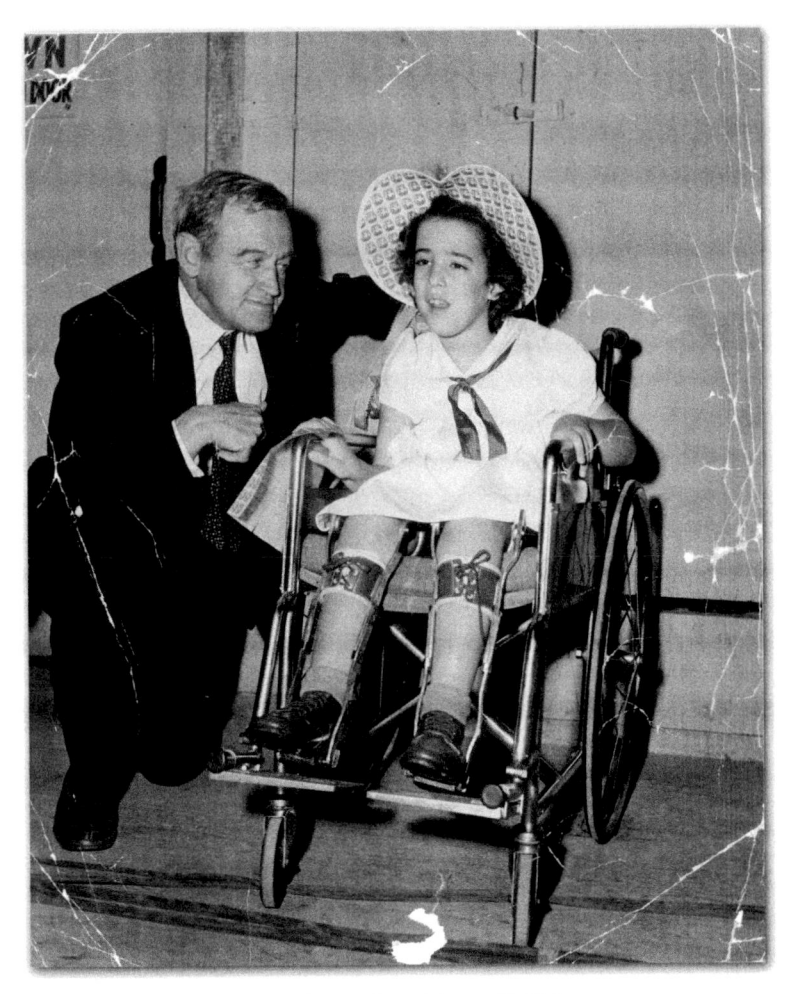

Patty in her Easter Seals hat with actor Barry Fitzgerald, 1948

Life Just Isn't Fair

Dad, Patty and Mom, 1939

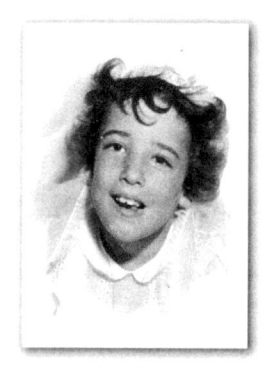

Patty on her first
Communion Day, 1947

Dad and Patty, 1943

Patty in her Sombrero
from Panama, 1943

Patty at Casa Colina after surgery
to her knees and ankles, 1945

Chapter 12

Camarillo State Hospital— A Trip Into Hell

Camarillo State Hospital, 1950

Mike's Chapter

Entering the grounds of Camarillo State Hospital back in the 1960s always was a frightening experience for a 19-year-old boy. I never completely got the image of the place out of my mind. I remember being very much on edge as I was ushered through the hallways, hearing the metal security doors closing behind me. On some occasions I would encounter a female patient, completely undressed and in a catatonic state, wandering down the hallways seemingly with no connection at all to the world she lived in.

My trips to the hospital were to visit our dear sister Patty, born with cerebral palsy, who had been committed to Camarillo in 1958 after a complete breakdown at our home in Hawthorne, California. This state mental hospital did not seem to me like the proper facility for Patty but at the time and without significant financial resources, it was my parents' only option.

In an amazing turn of events, our mother, who suffered from manic-depressive illness most of her life, had a breakdown in the spring of 1960 and, in accordance with her own wishes, she was committed to Camarillo State Hospital. For a brief period of time, Mother and Patty were both patients at this very intimidating institution. I don't know how our father maintained his sanity. Having the two people whom he loved most in his life as patients in this hell-hole at the same time had to be devastating and at times hard to comprehend. Dad had amazing resilience and somehow kept the Thornton family together both financially and emotionally.

Camarillo State Hospital, located three miles south of the city of Camarillo, a beautiful little town just a few miles from the Pacific Ocean, appeared very tranquil and serene on the outside. On the inside, it was anything but. During the 1950s and 1960s, the

Camarillo State Hospital—A Trip into Hell

Camarillo hospital housed the largest population of mentally ill people in the country. At its peak, 7,000 patients were housed in this facility, which on the outside looked more like a resort in Mexico than a hospital.

The city of Camarillo in the 1950s was an area primarily of orange, lemon and avocado orchards with only about 4,000 residents, mostly Hispanic. Agriculture was the primary source of income in Ventura County and although we had only three acres of lemons, we belonged to the Sunkist Lemon Association in Oxnard. Lemons yield about eight crops per year and periodically we would receive a small check.

In June of 1958, when I graduated from Junipero Serra High School in Gardena, California, and received the signing bonus from the Los Angeles Dodgers and with Patty then in Camarillo State Hospital, putting a portion of this money into the three acres of lemons seemed like a good idea.

According to the L.A. Weekly of November 2002, "Camarillo opened in 1936 and by the 1950s was home to more than 7,000 alcoholics, pedophiles, and people with mental illness, retardation and violent propensities. It housed almost as many nurses, doctors and hospital workers. Throughout the next several decades, it occupied a central place in the coastal communities of Ventura County, not only as a source of employment but also as a destination for families that relocated to be closer to relatives committed to the hospital."

That is exactly why the Thornton clan sold their home in Hawthorne and moved to Camarillo in 1959, to be closer to our dear sister and daughter, Patty.

The newspaper account continued, "The subject of myths, novels, film and song, Camarillo closed its doors in 1997, after President Reagan's de-institutionalization policy finally rendered it obsolete, leaving behind a unique place in the community and a disturbing history of institutional care."

She Loved Everyone But Me

It's impossible to provide a thorough history of the Thornton family without mentioning Camarillo State Hospital. Patty lived there for nine years and Mother was a patient there for several months in the 1960s. After having Patty home with us for 19 years, it was very painful and disturbing to have to accept the fact that this was her new home. We visited there hundreds of times over the years and it was always hard to see Patty as belonging with this rather disturbed group of people who resided at Camarillo State Hospital. Our dear sister was an angel and she always had the ability to see the good in people and somehow this helped her to make the best of her situation. After she left Camarillo State Hospital, the various institutions and nursing homes Patty lived in until her death at age 63 all were far superior in every way to Camarillo.

In 1964, about a year and a half after we were married, my wife Sheryl and I moved back to Camarillo from Idaho. For Sheryl, born and raised in Idaho, this was her first time living in California. I had been living in Twin Falls, Idaho, off and on since 1961 and was looking forward to returning to the beautiful Camarillo area and being close to Patty and my folks again.

Sheryl and I frequently brought Patty home on Sundays for a barbecue at Mom and Dad's house. She was always thrilled to see us and, of course, a good meal was definitely one of the joys of Patty's unfortunate life. The girl loved to eat!

When I describe Patty's life as being unfortunate, that is a comment made from my perspective and not Patty's. I might have seen her life as being quite sad at times but Patty was usually upbeat and happy even under the most difficult of circumstances, like having to spend nine years of her life in Camarillo State Hospital.

It was always difficult for me when Sheryl and I would take Patty back to the hospital after our having had a nice day together. Upon entering the wards, the illusion created by the beautiful

Camarillo State Hospital—A Trip into Hell

Spanish architecture and the lovely grounds was extinguished. There was, instead, the dreadful reality of the sights and sounds and smells of insanity. Standing in the dayroom of one of the women's wards, looking around me, and seeing the bizarre clothes worn by the patients, their odd mannerisms, their agitated pacing, strange laughter and their occasional heartbreaking screams was a vision that would be clearly etched in my mind for all time.

A large percentage of the patients at Camarillo were either in a drug-induced catatonic state, walking the hallways with a blank stare on their faces, or they would be rambling on and on about nothing in particular, carrying on imaginary conversations with the characters who populated their own make-believe world.

Many of the ladies of all ages on Patty's ward would want to come close to me and sometimes touch me, not necessarily in a sexual way, but almost as if I might have reminded them of a son or a husband and the loving relationship that, on occasion, they were capable of remembering. It was a sad and strange world inside the walls of Camarillo State Hospital.

Much of the unusual behavior of most of these patients was due to large doses of psychotropic drugs used, I think excessively, to control them. Over time, these drugs take a devastating toll on the victims.

It was a great day in all of our lives when Patty moved to Idaho in 1967 and the Thornton family was able to put Camarillo State Hospital in the past where it became a distant memory. We were so accustomed to chaos in our lives that we accepted Camarillo State Hospital as just another part of that.

Mother's lifelong struggle with mental illness was something she just couldn't overcome. She was extremely self-conscious about what she thought it implied, that she was a weak person and was continually letting the family down. During the 1940s and the 1950s, most people had no understanding of mental illness and didn't realize that it was a sickness like any other that had to be treated with drugs and therapy. At the time, many people didn't want to tell anyone that they had a family member in Camarillo. The stigma was too great.

It's ironic that Camarillo State Hospital which opened its doors in 1936 and would become home to thousands upon thousands of alcoholics, pedophiles and people with mental illness would shut down in 1997 and re-open in 2002 as a respected institution of higher learning. It became the 23rd addition to the California State University system and was called Cal State Channel Islands. The University is offering its students academic programs focusing on Liberal Studies, Science and Business. What an amazing transformation!!

She Loved Everyone But Me

Dad at the lemon grove, 1959

Mom proudly displaying
a Thornton Lemon, 1959

Celebrating Patty's
21st birthday, October 1959

Mom decked out in
Mike's Doger uniform, 1959

111

Camarillo State Hospital—A Trip into Hell

Camarillo State Hospital, 1950

Chapter 13

What a Difference a Day Makes

Bill and Kathy on their
Wedding Day,
May 6, 1961

Kathy's Chapter

December 18, 1958, was a fateful day for the Thornton Family. That was the day I met my future husband, Bill Crow, from Twin Falls, Idaho. He was visiting my next door neighbor, Shirley Black, and I had buzzed over to borrow some cream of tartar for cookies I was making for my senior year Christmas dance at Marymount. Three years later Bill and I were married and living in Twin Falls.

Within the next six years, all of my family members, Mom, Dad, Patty, Mike and Colleen would re-locate to Twin Falls, one or two at a time. The person this migration impacted the most was Patty. Her life had taken a decidedly downhill slide in 1958 when she was diagnosed with schizo-affective disorder, a genetic cousin to Mother's bi-polar illness, and placed in Camarillo State Mental Hospital.

Her move to Idaho in 1967 removed Patty from the chaotic environment of that institution and into a series of nursing homes, which she much preferred. Her final six years were spent in an Assisted Living Facility, The Main Street House, in Jerome, Idaho, where she lived with seven other disabled men and women. She had finally come full circle, living in a home once again, helping with the cooking and other household chores and getting out into the community on a daily basis. She absolutely loved it!

The move to Idaho had been a real positive for Mother as well. Another chance at a new beginning seemed to rekindle in her an enjoyment of life that had been missing for several years during which time she had spent much of each day in bed. She was suffering from a deep depression but now refused the electroshock treatments that had pulled her out of it in the past.

This period was a very difficult one not only for Mother but also for Dad and Colleen, who was the only child living at home at this point. Both Mother and Dad had doted on Colleen from the time she was born in 1949. When our Uncle Emmett and Aunt Louise came to our home to meet Colleen shortly after her birth, Dad took them into our parents' bedroom to see the sleeping baby. Emmett came out of the bedroom exclaiming, "You'd think it was his first child the way he's carrying on about that baby!"

Raising Colleen was a much more leisurely parenting experience than the hectic one Mother and Dad had known with their first three stair-step children. They got a big kick out of everything Colleen did and, in their minds, she could do no wrong.

Imagine the shock to this adored child when, at the age of 12, she was pretty much left to fend for herself six days a week until Dad got home late after completing his Helms Bakery route. She went from being the center of attention for both her parents to feeling quite alone in life. She was embarrassed to bring friends home because of concerns about Mother's behavior. By her own admission to me, these difficult years erased from her memory all recollection of the good times she had shared with Mother. Dad became her hero and confidant. Colleen felt that she had been abandoned by Mom and she was never able to totally forgive her or forget the emotional pain she had experienced. As a result, Colleen does not see Mother in the same light as Mike, Patty and I.

By the time Colleen was born, Patty was ten and a half years old. Our younger sister missed out on those early years when Mother's dedication and devotion to Patty were so inspirational to the rest of the family. That fact plus the negative experiences during her teen years make it completely understandable why Colleen's perspective is so different from Mike's and mine. Nonetheless, her bad memories did not deter Colleen from becoming a devoted caregiver to Mother in her declining years.

Putting this sad period behind her and resuming an active lifestyle after the move to Twin Falls was such a blessing for Mother. She and Dad settled into a contented existence and thoroughly enjoyed exploring the beautiful outdoors that seduces everyone who comes to Idaho. Fishing together in Hagerman Valley became their favorite pastime.

Mental illness is a stealthy adversary, however, and in the spring of 1970 Mother unexpectedly had another breakdown. It was a Saturday afternoon in May and I was putting the finishing touches on my daughter, Cindy's, First Communion dress when the phone rang. It was my frantic father on the line telling me that Mother was on her way to the bus station and was planning to leave town for who knows where. I immediately called Dr. Kenneth Briggs, a local psychiatrist we had recently consulted about Mother's increasingly bizarre behavior. His advice to me was to call the police department, explain to them that my mother was in the throes of a mental breakdown and needed to be stopped from leaving town on the Greyhound bus. The policeman instructed me to meet him at the bus station where I pointed out Mother sitting comfortably in the back of the bus. He entered the bus, asked Mother to please accompany him, which she did rather dejectedly, and we all headed for Magic Valley Regional Medical Center. There we met Dr. Briggs and he committed Mother to the mental unit.

I will never forget that day. It was like an out-of-body experience. I couldn't believe it was really happening. The good news is — it was the last breakdown my mother ever experienced! Dr. Briggs introduced her to a new psychotropic drug called Lithium, which modifies the severity of the highs and lows that bi-polar patients experience and moves them into a much more even-tempered existence. The loss for the medicated person is the excitement that life brought them during the early stages of their manic periods. As a result, Lithium was a mixed blessing for Mother. She lived another 29 years and never again had the frightening experience of succumbing to a severe mental

What a Difference a Day Makes

breakdown but gone, too, was much of the vibrancy of her personality. Her life would never again be as exhilarating but neither would it be so terrifying. Life is full of trade-offs for all of us and Mother had chosen hers.

For the relatives and friends of people who take Lithium, many of the traits that made their loved ones exciting, endearing and fun to know are muted or disappear. As Dr. Kay Redfield Jamison so aptly put it in her autobiographical book, *An Unquiet Mind*, "there is now a rather bittersweet exchange of a comfortable and settled present existence for a troubled but immensely lived past." I have often bemoaned the fact that many of my mother's younger grandchildren never knew the "real" Grandma Thornton but in 1970 Mother willingly made the "bittersweet exchange" and never looked back.

Chapter 14

Lithium: The Miracle Drug

Bob and Eileen at their 50th Anniversary Celebration, June 22, 1988

Mike's Chapter

Mother had her last major breakdown in Twin Falls, Idaho, in 1970. She had boarded a bus and was headed for parts unknown, but the police were able to stop the bus before it departed Twin Falls and thus interrupt her plans. We asked Dr. Kenneth Briggs, a psychiatrist based in Twin Falls, to advise us on how we should treat Mother's illness. His recommendation proved to be a major turning point in Mother's life.

Dr. Briggs told us about a new experimental drug called Lithium. Lithium, thank God, gave Mother many years of relative peace. She never had another major incident in her life and despite her refusal to have her blood analyzed on a regular basis to control the levels of Lithium in her system, the side effects of the drug were manageable. While it gave stability to her life and peace to her mind, the use of Lithium and many other drugs over many years definitely robbed Mother of her once dynamic and exciting personality.

Lithium, the mineral, is a simple, naturally occurring salt. The lithium that is used in both medicine and industry comes mainly from rocks and brine. It is the 31st most abundant element on earth. Less than nine percent of all lithium mined is for pharmaceutical use. Medical Lithium is always used in the form of salt either lithium carbonate or lithium citrate. The effective component is the lithium ion. It was first used as a treatment for mania by Carl Lange of Denmark and William Hammond of New York in the late 1800s. By the early 1900s it was no longer an accepted therapy and did not experience a renaissance until John Cade from Australia started treating patients with it in 1949. The United States Food and Drug Administration did not approve Lithium for patients who suffered from mania until 1970. The

Lithium: The Miracle Drug

main reason it took so long for widespread acceptance of this drug was that overdosing sometimes resulted in death. This is why blood levels of patients on Lithium therapy need to be tested regularly in order to maintain an appropriate level.

Psychotropic drugs all have side effects. Because Lithium is most effective during the manic phase of bi-polar illness, Mother also took the anti-depressant, Mellaril. The main side effect of this drug for Mother was hand tremors which made it almost impossible for her to drink out of a glass. Her hands shook to such an extent that for many years she had to use a straw for consuming liquids. At the time, everyone, including Mother, felt that these tremors from Mellaril and the muting of her personality from Lithium were minor inconveniences in comparison to her many years of successive nervous breakdowns and the resulting general chaos visited upon her and her entire family.

Mother took her medication faithfully for over 20 years but I don't believe she had her blood levels of Lithium checked consistently to keep the drug at the levels that would provide her with the best quality of life possible and protect her from the lethal potential of this powerful drug. I don't think she ever fully comprehended how vitally important a component of Lithium therapy the blood tests are. Determining just the right drug levels is an issue for many people who are plagued with bi-polar illness.

Dr. Kay Redfield Jamison, who is one of the foremost authorities on this illness, also has experienced it firsthand. For many years, as she pursued a career in academic medicine, she found herself experiencing the same exhilarating highs and catastrophic lows that afflicted many of her patients. This resulted in her engaging in wild spending sprees, violence and even attempting suicide.

In her best selling book, *An Unquiet Mind*, Dr. Jamison recounts a conversation she had with her significant other. She says, "I told him about my problems with the idea of taking

She Loved Everyone But Me

Lithium, but also that my life was dependent on it. I told him that I had discussed with my psychiatrist the possibility of taking a lower dose in hopes of alleviating some of the more problematic side affects. I was eager to do this, but very frightened that I would have a recurrence of my mania."

Dr. Jamison continues, "after discussing it with my psychiatrist in Los Angeles and my doctor in London, I did very slowly cut back on the amount of Lithium I was taking. The effect was dramatic. It was as though I had taken bandages off my eyes after many years of partial blindness. A few days after lowering my dose, I was walking in Hyde Park along the side of the serpentine, when I realized that my steps were literally bouncier than they had been and that I was taking in sights and sounds that had previously been filtered through thick layers of gauze. The quacking of the ducks was more insistent, clearer and more intense; the bumps on the sidewalk were far more noticeable; I felt more energetic and alive. Most significant, I could once again read without effort. It was in short, remarkable."

We'll never know what might have been. Mother was a very stubborn person and once she made up her mind that she wasn't going to do something there was no changing her mind. I don't believe that during the almost 25 years that she was taking Lithium, Mother, a previously voracious reader, ever read a book. She was unable to concentrate on anything for an extended period of time.

The price that patients with mental illness have to pay because of the use of psychotropic drugs gives some insight into how devastating these illnesses can be. In 1992 Mother suffered from severe stroke-like symptoms that resulted in her being given a vast array of tests and necessitated a stay at the Elks Rehabilitation Center in Boise. It was eventually determined that she had experienced a toxic reaction to Lithium and was at that time switched to the anticonvulsant, Depakote, a drug that recently had been accepted as another effective treatment for mania. It would become the most prescribed drug (surpassing Lithium) for treating manic episodes associated with bi-polar disorder. Depakote served Mother well until she passed away in 1999. It was and is incredibly painful for me to think about her life. One of my biggest disappointments is that my children never knew the person that Mother really was.

I remember that during my school years from about seventh grade through my senior year in high school, I couldn't wait to get home from school, particularly when Mother was well. If something good had happened that day, I knew that Mom would not only be as excited as I was but I would have her undivided attention as I told her about it. What a terrific feeling for any young person to know that they have the support of a parent and that someone will be waiting when they get home to listen to the events of their day! It was a significant part of the exceptional relationship I always had with Mother.

My mother was a great listener and we could probably all improve on that trait in ourselves. As parents, we frequently are too quick to critique what our kids are telling us, offering too many suggestions and often criticism, when what they really need the most at that time is somebody to just listen.

Dr. Leo Buscaglia, the enormously popular lecturer and professor at the University of Southern California, now deceased, tells about an incident that occurred while he was on a flight from Los Angeles to New York. When he boarded the plane the stewardess shouted with delight.

"I've wanted to meet you for such a long time," she said, "May I talk to you later?"

When she got a break, she sat next to me and frantically told her story which involved a cheating husband, a disturbed child, a feeling of despondency and hopelessness, a fear of being unable to cope.

After a long while, according to Dr. Buscaglia, the stewardess stopped in mid-sentence and sighed deeply with relief. She wiped her tears and sat up in the seat.

"Oh Dr. Buscaglia," she said, "You've helped me so much."

Dr. Buscaglia tells us, "I hadn't said a word."

Sometimes helping can be just listening, without judgment or advice. Mother had a wonderful ability to do just that, particularly early on, before she was stabilized but changed by Lithium.

Chapter 15

"Oh, Bosh!"

Eileen
1932

Kathy's Chapter

"Oh, bosh!" was an expression that sprang freely from Mother's lips whenever she was confronted with mendacity, gossip or nonsense. As an adult, I have often wondered if this expression was not a euphemism from back in the day for a more earthy exclamation, which never would have escaped Mother's lips. She did not mind an occasional "damn" or "hell" but anything beyond that was anathema to her. As she used to admonish us kids, "There are too many good words in the English language without resorting to the vernacular of the streets."

Among the expressions that peppered Mother's speech, I have a few favorites that I particularly associate with her. Mother never had much tolerance for gossip and she had some sound advice for those who engaged in it. "There's so much good in the worst of us and so much bad in the best of us, that it ill behooves any of us to talk about the rest of us."

Mother's reply to the offer of a second helping at mealtime was, "I've had an elegant sufficiency, thank you."

There were occasional loud thunderstorms during the California winters and her reaction to them was, "The angels must be rearranging the furniture in heaven." This expression added a nice, light touch to what could have been a frightening experience for a young child.

Some of Mother's sayings have a kind of old-fashioned ring to them and I suspect she may have picked them up from her own Mother. And now, I find myself using them occasionally with my children.

My favorite memory of my mother is how special it was to have her always there to talk with when I came home from school. I can see her still, carrying her Lazy Susan containing a pot of tea and

"Oh Bosh!"

some fresh baked cookies and putting it down on our round, maple coffee table before she settled in on the sofa for a cozy chat about the happenings of the day. She always made me feel as if my news was the most interesting thing she had heard all day. It was during those chats that many of the afore-mentioned sayings came into play as well as one she used whenever someone she loved was mistreated, "Just consider the source, dear," she counseled. The memory that has stayed with me my whole life is knowing how much she cared for me, how she made time for me and how she always wanted the best for all her children.

These happy memories of Mother have not overshadowed the negative events that were part and parcel of having a parent with a bi-polar condition. Etched in my memory are the scary times when I felt as though my mother had been taken over by a monster, which indeed she had — the monster of mental illness. It was then I would think, "This is not my real mom. This is the person who takes over her mind and body when she's sick. Soon my real mom will be back and everything will be fine."

These were my thoughts when I came home from high school one afternoon and noticed that the living room curtains were missing. I walked through the living room and into the kitchen and those windows were also bare. Just as I was thinking that Mom must have washed the curtains today, I looked out the kitchen window into the backyard and there were all the curtains and curtain rods strewn across the lawn. I turned to my left and there was Mother, standing in front of the kitchen sink. She was drinking a glass of tomato juice.

Puzzled I walked over to her and said, "Mother, why are all the curtains in the backyard?"

"None of your damn business," she replied as she threw her glass of tomato juice all over me.

That night the ambulance came and took Mother to the hospital for more shock treatments. Mother didn't talk much about shock

She Loved Everyone But Me

treatments except to say she was afraid of them, she hated them. She was sure she'd had at least thirty of them in her adult life. Based on the number of breakdowns she had, I think it was probably more. She once told me that she could feel when her manic spells were coming on. It was very frightening to her as there was nothing she could do to stop them. She said she felt like she was on a runaway train heading for disaster. At the end of the train wreck waited the despised shock treatments. When she came home from the hospital after receiving the treatments, she'd be very quiet, almost catatonic, for a while. This period was very eerie and worrisome for us children. We would try everything to cheer her up, jokes, funny stories, good behavior and anything else we could think up. Gradually, over time, like a butterfly from its cocoon, her old personality would emerge and we'd have our mother back.

When I watched the movie, *A Beautiful Mind*, about Nobel Prize winner, John Nash, who unfortunately suffered from schizophrenia, I became painfully aware of why my mother so despised shock therapy. In this film there is a graphic depiction of John Nash receiving an electroshock treatment. His arms and legs are strapped down, a tongue protector is placed in his mouth and his body shakes violently as the electricity strikes him. This was a horrifying and emotional scene for me to witness and it still haunts me to this day. Every time it comes to mind, I visualize my mother strapped to that bed and experiencing what John Nash experienced. It seems so barbaric. It makes me cry.

"Bi-polar" is a very descriptive term for the illness that plagued my mother. It conveys the two extremes, manic and depressive, that characterize the actions of the men and women who suffer from this disorder. Those who live with manic-depressive people visit these extremes with their afflicted loved ones and ride the tides of elation and despair that are intrinsic to their lives. Being with Mother when she was soaring through the early stages of her manic highs was great fun. She was intelligent, loquacious, fun-loving and

"Oh Bosh!"

full of stories. She possessed an intense and infectious joie de vivre. Watching her ultimate plunge into the depths of irrationality and despair was as heart-wrenching as the early stages were exciting and fun.

Mother received a tremendous boost to her self-confidence when it became known to the public in the 1970s that the vast majority of mental illnesses, including bi-polar illness, were caused chiefly by chemical imbalances in the body. For most of her adult life well-meaning friends and family members would on occasion make comments to her such as, "It's no wonder you have these breakdowns, Eileen, what with Patty's handicaps to deal with."

Far from being comforting, these statements were very troubling to Mother as they implied either that she was weak and incapable of dealing with difficulties or that her beloved Patty was somehow responsible for her breakdowns. Neither explanation appealed to her in the least.

As a result Mother developed the habit of always saying she was "fine" no matter what was going on in her life. Through her own illnesses, Patty's problems, Dad's drinking, as well as a mine field of illnesses that were exploding all around her in her later years, as far as she was concerned, she was always "fine, thank you."

One of the poignant parts of human communication is that the messages we send are not always the ones that are received. Many friends and family members came to see Mom's assertions that she was always "fine" as a sign of her being out of touch with reality, at best, or in some instances as heartless, at worst. This was particularly true when my father passed away. Mother came across to some as not displaying an appropriate amount of grief at this sad time. What she was trying to communicate in this instance, as well as at many other times in her life when she was misunderstood, was, "I can handle this crisis. I'm not weak. I'm strong. I won't crack under the strain of this."

Even in those years when breakdowns became a thing of the

She Loved Everyone But Me

past, Mom continued to display her "I'm fine" façade. Old habits die hard!

Just how deeply saddened Mother was by the loss of her best friend became abundantly clear to the family at the Thanksgiving Day celebration one month after Dad's death. After our meal, everyone retired to the living room to get comfortable and converse. We were all chatting away when around the corner from the kitchen came Mother. A very clear "Let's go, Bob" rang out. We all sat there in shock and the look on Mother's face spoke volumes. The depth of her grief permeated the room as it dawned on her that her beloved Bob was not there to take her home.

Can happiness be found in a household where mental illness, alcoholism and cerebral palsy co-exist? To those whose idea of a happy family is two adults, mother and father, both with fulfilling careers, two healthy children, a large, comfortable home and an annual family vacation including, at least once, the mandatory pilgrimage to Disneyland, the answer would most likely be an emphatic No! My own answer to that question would be an emphatic Yes! So many wonderful qualities that my parents, Bob and Eileen Thornton, had overrode the negatives and made living with them a joy and a blessing. In addition to my mom always having an open ear when I came home from school and my dad being a "playing daddy", other aspects of their personalities provide many fond memories.

For instance, my mom was a great cook. The interesting thing is she had seldom cooked before she was married. No one taught her how to cook. She never used recipes. Everything was in her head. Memories of Thanksgiving dinners with her savory corn bread dressing as well as her delicious lasagna and spaghetti, her spicy enchiladas and special Sunday ham make my mouth water still. She also loved to bake. Her lemon meringue pies, marshmallow cake and ranger cookies are unmatched by any I have ever tasted.

When I look back on our Thanksgiving celebrations, which

"Oh Bosh!"

were always enhanced by the huge turkey Uncle Ide had raised for us, what I always remember with a chuckle is my brother, Mike, living up to Mother's saying, "Your eyes are bigger than your stomach." Mike would gorge himself on all of Mom's scrumptious holiday dishes and then stagger away from the table and into his bed for a two-hour nap.

One problem we children had when we got older and started doing our own cooking was since she never had followed any recipes, it was difficult, if not impossible, to duplicate Mom's wonderful dishes.

As for Dad, he had a very creative mind and loved to do artistic things. This manifested itself in many different ways from drawing cartoon characters and helping me decorate the brown paper covers the nuns mandated for our school books to meticulously decorating the Christmas tree down to the last strand of perfectly hung tinsel. His artistry also manifested itself in his beautiful stone work that gained him the reputation of being one of the best masons in Southern California.

One of mother's favorite stories about Dad was of the first Easter we spent in our new home on 140th Street. It seems our parents had stayed up to the wee hours of the morning preparing Easter baskets for their offspring. Dad had colored and hand-painted six eggs for each of us. Before going to bed, they had filled all our Easter baskets with the beautiful eggs as well as an assortment of Easter candy. Then they lovingly placed each of the baskets by our beds. The next morning Mother and Dad were eagerly anticipating the delighted looks on their children's faces when they saw their special baskets. Well, since Mike and I had not been up half the night, we jumped out of bed early Easter morning and by the time Mom and Dad awakened, all the carefully painted eggs had been peeled and what remained of the yolks were all in Mike's basket and what remained of the whites were in mine! This definitely went down as one of the most disappointing experiences

She Loved Everyone But Me

our dad had as a young father.

Dad loved to garden and this hobby revealed his artistic skills as well. He was the first person I knew who gardened in raised beds. He would plant vine crops like squash and cucumbers in round raised beds and other vegetables such as corn and green beans in rectangular ones. His gardens made a beautiful mosaic. In his later years, he had a rose garden that was the talk of the neighborhood. Mother delighted in the beautiful, colorful bouquets he would bring her after laboring in his roses each summer day. My dad definitely had the proverbial green thumb.

One of Mother's talents, which brought great joy to her life, was her ability to sing and play the piano. She was never happier than when we'd take a Sunday drive to her brother Jack's acreage in West Covina. Once there, we'd all gather around the piano and Mother would play and we'd all sing, belting out every Irish song in our repertoire.

Mother loved to laugh and had a great sense of fun. She was always ready for a good time but she hated games — card games, board games — she never wanted to play them. One summer our next door neighbors taught Mike and me how to play Canasta. We loved it and were determined that the first chance we got we would talk Mother into playing with us. Dad left for work early as usual that day and we four kids were sitting around the kitchen table finishing up breakfast when Mike started in on Mom.

His closer statement was, "Come on, Mom just one hand and if you don't like it, we'll quit."

Well, we didn't quit. We played all morning, stopped for a quick lunch, played all afternoon and were still going strong when Dad arrived home around six. His eyes bulged out of his head when he saw us all sitting there at the table in our pajamas, just as he'd left us that morning. The thing that surprised Dad the most about the whole scene was that we had talked Mother into playing cards! What a fun day! It was Mother's first and last game of Canasta.

"Oh Bosh!"

Mother loved Idaho's Snake River Canyon and, in her later years, we would often take drives down to the canyon. She never once failed to exclaim about how gorgeous it was and how she thought most Idahoans took it for granted.

"Why, Shoshone Falls is more beautiful than Niagara," she would say, "and no one around here seems to appreciate it."

On one of our drives shortly after Dad died, Mom and I were reminiscing about him and, along with so many of his good qualities, she talked about his drinking problem. I asked her why she hadn't been harder on him over his drinking. Her answer impressed on me how grateful she was to Dad.

She said, "Kathy, how many men would have stayed with me like your father did? I considered it a matter of loyalty. I put up with his shortcomings just as he put up with mine."

Recently my husband, Bill, and I were listening to a Teaching Company lecture series on the life of Winston Churchill, the World War II British leader who with steely determination almost single-handedly rallied the British people to victory and "their finest hour." While Hitler was making his relentless march of conquest across Europe and many leaders in England were advocating appeasement, Churchill encouraged his people to stand up to Hitler, defend their island nation and in the process save western civilization as we know it.

In this audio series the story is told of Churchill being asked in his declining years to give the commencement address at Harrow, the boarding school he attended as a boy. Churchill's exhortation to these graduates consisted of only six words, "Never give up, never, never, never!"

My thoughts when I heard this went immediately to my mother. It suddenly came to me. This is what I admired most about her. In spite of all she had endured in her life, she never gave up. She always looked forward to each new day and assumed it was going to be a happy one.

She Loved Everyone But Me

It is not my intention to imply that Mother was a perfect person or a living saint for she was not. Like all us humans, she had her faults, chiefly a tendency toward impulsive actions and blunt speech. I do not believe these faults arose from a meanness of spirit but rather a lack of awareness of how her words and actions sometimes affected those around her. Where she thought she was being helpful, she was sometimes hurtful. I must confess to losing my patience at times when Mother would blurt out something that hurt my feelings but I always tried to remind myself later of all she had done for me personally, always taking time to listen to me and always showering me with love and support in spite of the demands of maintaining a household of six people as well as taking care of the many needs of a handicapped child.

Mother spent the last thirty days of her life at Magic Valley Regional Medical Center. She had developed pneumonia due to an inability to eat without aspirating her food into her lungs. Her doctors thought she would be gone in a week, but she hung on, thinking that any day she was going to get better. When I asked her during the second week of her hospital stay if she was ready to go be with Dad, she replied, "Heavens, no!"

She still had some fight left in her. She was determined to live out her life as best she could for as long as she could. It remains a marvel to me that she made it to the ripe old age of eighty-six in spite of all she had dealt with in her life, which included in her later years: surgery, radiation and chemotherapy for colon cancer, radioactive iodine treatment for hyperthyroidism and severe, debilitating, stroke-like reactions to her psycho-tropic medicines. When she was seventy-nine she lost her husband of fifty-three years and was left with a tremendous void in her life.

Through it all she just kept on keeping on. She never gave up on herself. She never gave up on her marriage. She never gave up on helping Patty. She never gave up, never, never, never!

Chapter 16

Queen or Oscar?

Michael Thornton
Dancing with
Grandma Eileen
1986

Kathy's Chapter

There is an old saying that goes something like this: "We are all three people: we are who we are; we are who we think we are and we are who other people think we are." Regarding the third part of this saying as it pertains to Mother and the thinking of her grandchildren, the opinions run the gamut from describing her as a Queen to comparing her to Oscar of *The Odd Couple* film fame.

Colleen's son, John, who is in management with Amazon.com in Seattle, eulogized his grandmother with these words:

"As anyone who met Grandma Thornton would attest, she was an extremely unique person that even the most casual acquaintance would not easily forget.

"As a child, I remember Grandma deciding in an instant that she was ready to go home from a family party. She would call for Grandpa and inform him that she was leaving with or without him. I remember wondering how she was planning to get home without Grandpa since she didn't drive!

"I remember slumber parties with Grandma and Grandpa. I remember watching Dale Murphy and the Atlanta Braves. Grandma used to tell me, 'John, that Dale Murphy is a fine, young gentleman.' Grandma had a soft spot in her heart for gentlemen. I can see why she married Grandpa.

"Grandma and Grandpa took me fishing in Hagerman during the summers. She would sit on the bank with a big sun hat on and watch Grandpa and me catch our limit. She informed me that she didn't fish anymore but she had been a great fisherman.

"In describing Grandma, the word opinionated immediately comes to mind. Whether Grandma was telling Michelle that her hair looked terrible or she thought the person next to her had some problems, she would tell you. I enjoyed bringing my friends to visit

Queen or Oscar?

Grandma and watching her size them up and determining whether she liked them or not. Eye contact, manners and being Irish were good. A lack of eye contact, long, straight hair and not being Irish were bad!

"Grandma gave a lot more to the world than her 'Oh, Bob' and 'Bosh' statements. To get a sense of who she was and what her impact was on the world, just take a look around the church. She is directly responsible for the lives of so many of us here today. She raised four wonderful children, who raised ten wonderful grandchildren, who are currently raising I don't know how many wonderful great-grandchildren.

"Grandma impacted my life by the way she taught Uncle Mike, Aunt Pat, Aunt Kathy and my mother how to be excellent people. The way her children cared for her the past few years and months speaks volumes about them and her. Although Grandma has left the world and moved on to a better place, her spirit will live on through her children and their families."

My daughter, Suzanne, who is a medical transcriptionist in Twin Falls, had a special relationship with her Aunt Pat. This affinity evolved from the fact that their birthdays were just three days apart and they would often have joint celebrations.

Suzanne was also a very faithful visitor to both her aunt and her grandmother during their later years when visits from their family members became a special blessing to both of them. Suzie has commented that during her visits when they both lived at the Twin Falls Care Center, "Grandma and Aunt Pat reminded me of Oscar and Felix because just like in the movie, *The Odd Couple*, an observer could tell the two of them were crazy about one another but they wouldn't leave each other alone. This observation stemmed from the fact that Mother continued to try to perfect Patty throughout her life. Even when Patty was into her sixties, admonitions like "sit up straight" and "don't talk with your mouth full" sprang from Mother's lips on a regular basis, much to Patty's

She Loved Everyone But Me

chagrin. And, as many grown children do, Patty had all kinds of unsolicited advice for her mother such as, "Why do you always say you feel fine? I can tell you don't feel well today. Just admit it."

In spite of this haranguing bantering between them, as Suzie observed, they loved each other dearly. Patty's favorite nickname for Mother during these later years was "my little peach."

Mike's son, Michael, who is a golf professional in Boise, offered a very insightful observation about his grandmother while we were chatting last Christmas. He said that he enjoyed her more when he visited her in her home than when he saw her at family gatherings. He observed that she was much more relaxed and talkative during his visits, always very solicitous, anxious to fix a good dinner for him and have him watch the Atlanta Braves ball game with her and Grandpa. It was during these visits Michael realized that not only was his grandmother happier and more fun in a one-on-one social situation but also what a great cook she was.

Mother truly was a one-on-one person. She definitely was more in her element visiting with people one or two at a time. It was then that her story-telling skills came to the fore. My daughter, Tammy, who is a fifth grade teacher in Pullman, Washington, once described how much she enjoyed visiting with her grandmother when she was on breaks from college.

"We would talk for hours," she said. "I would tell Grandma all about school and she would tell me stories like how Grandpa stroked her fur coat or how she got caught at a speakeasy during Prohibition. She always gave me great advice about men. She would say, 'Now, Tammy, don't be in any great hurry to get married. You've got plenty of time. He has to be the right one and you have to be able to talk openly to one another'."

Mother reveled in the opportunity for get-togethers such as the ones Michael and Tammy have described.

Mike's oldest daughter, Kecia, who is an R. N. and manages a surgical clinic in Portland, Oregon, recently sent me the following

Queen or Oscar?

commentary on her Grandmother.

"'Bob, we're leaving!' those words signaled that my Grandmother Thornton had grown tired at a family event and was ready to go home. She would stand up, always perfectly dressed and usually wearing a matching hat and all the grandchildren and children would politely kiss her goodbye as though she were the Queen.

"My Grandmother Thornton was what people call a character. She said and did funny things that she didn't intend to be funny, but actually were. She was not warm and fuzzy to me like my Grandmother Stevenson, who always made us homemade cookies. In fact, I don't have memories of anything homemade from Grandma Thornton as a child. She did make me several sandwiches though when I was attending nursing school as an adult.

"What she lacked in warmth, she made up for in mystery. She was my grandmother who grew up in Canada. She was the beautiful, slender, young blonde in the picture that any of us would have been proud to look like. She was the teenager who drove to the beach though she didn't know how to drive. She was the woman who married my Grandfather Thornton, who was actually born in Ireland. Even though she wasn't particularly warm to me as a child, I admired her because she was interesting.

"Grandmother Thornton was also my grandmother who was bi-polar. My parents never hid that from us kids. I assumed it was why she was the way she was. Grandma loves you but she's sometimes not very nice. That's what I grew up telling myself.

"When I was in nursing school, I made a decision to get to know her better. It was one of the best decisions I've made in my life. I would stop by their home after class every couple of weeks. They would usually be watching the Atlanta Braves on television or admiring my grandfather's beautiful rose garden. Spending one-on-one time with grandma allowed me to see that she was able to express her love to me in the right circumstances.

"You can't accurately describe my Grandma Thornton in words. Rather, she was a woman you had to experience. She was extremely mannered and poised. She carried herself with an air of confidence and pride. She could be quite blunt at times and she was definitely a no nonsense woman. In a different generation she would have made a fine businesswoman like her granddaughter today."

My daughter, Cindy, who is a graphic artist and home-schooling mom in Twin Falls, is the eldest of Mother's grandchildren and most likely the only one who has clear memories of her grandmother's pre-lithium days. She penned the following tribute to her grandmother when she died in 1999:

I can see you now, happy and smiling

No more struggle, no more strife.

You've finally crossed the finish line of life.

We, your family, can learn from you—

Never give up, whatever you do.

Try to be positive and the battle is won;

You're as young as you feel so keep thinking young.

Almighty God will see you through;

Stand by your family for their love is true.

These pointers for living

Are the treasure you leave behind,

And when I think of you, they will always come to mind.

Chapter 17

Don't Grieve for Me, For Now I'm Free

Mike, Kathy, Colleen and Patty, 1996 (the last picture of the four Thornton Siblings)

Mike & Kathy's Chapter

It's June 26, 2002, a beautiful sunny day in southern Idaho. The family has gathered at my "Brady Bunch" style home on Pierce Street in Twin Falls. The grandchildren are having a grand time, splashing and pushing each other in the pool. Their mothers and dads sit poolside tending their tots, but also catching up on all that has transpired since the last gathering of the clan. Their grandfathers, Mike and Bill, sit at the family room table catching up on the latest in the sports and political worlds but also casting an occasional glance out the windows to admire their offspring and laugh at their antics.

My generation of women, we 50 and 60-something's, are busy in the kitchen arranging all the delicious pot-luck dishes that have been brought, priding ourselves as our mothers did before us on what great cooks we all are! Nobody goes home hungry from a Thornton/Crow/Nemeth gathering. The air of festivity in this reunion belies the fact that we have just come from the cemetery where we laid to rest our dear sister, Patricia, who passed away quickly and quietly of a heart attack this week at the age of 63.

Lest anyone assume that we are heartless or indifferent, it is important to remember that ours is a predominately Irish family, more comfortable with a joyous Irish wake than an event with a more funereal spirit. And so we celebrate Patty's life. The underlying feelings are full of grief and sadness, since Patty's death was completely unexpected and none of us had the opportunity to say our final goodbyes. Named after St. Patrick herself, and never one to miss a family gathering, I could literally feel my sister Patty, looking down on this memorial get together and wishing she could join the fun.

Earlier, at Reynolds Funeral Chapel, Mike had given a touching eulogy to Patty, bringing alternately smiles to the lips and tears to the eyes of those present. The following is a summary of his remarks:

"It's remarkable that despite her physical limitations, Patty had such an incredible impact on so many lives. Patty never married, never had children, never held a job, didn't belong to any clubs or organizations, got a G.E.D. late in life, and yet so many people: nurses, doctors, family and friends felt so lucky to have known Patty and to have been a part of her life. She was an amazing person! Patty taught us all a valuable lesson about what was really important in our lives.

"Patty's life was a strong statement for the intrinsic value of human life. Born on October 11, 1938 in Los Angeles, California with a twin sister who died at birth, Patty survived and came into this world at a robust three pounds. She made up for that later in life! The girl loved to eat! She used to get so mad at Mother when Mother would tell her that she had to lose some weight. That was always a big bone of contention between Mother and Patty.

"Because she was born with cerebral palsy, Patty spent the next 63 years of her life dealing with the physical limitations of this affliction. For her first ten to twelve years, Mother and Dad were obsessed with Patty's developing the ability to walk. They'd put her leg braces on and have her try to walk between them. Theirs was a valiant effort made to get Patty to walk. She made some progress but was never able to walk independently. At eight years of age, she was chosen as the Easter Seal poster child. She was so cute! We have pictures of her with the famous actor of that time, Barry Fitzgerald, Patty proudly wearing her Easter Seals hat. That was one of the highlights of her young life.

"Every effort was made to have Patty receive a good education. She was sent to private school. The bus used to pick her up in front of the house. She also had a couple of teachers who came to the house for a number of years. Mother was determined that Patty was not going to be deprived of an education. She finally received her G.E.D. years later in Pocatello, Idaho, and was she ever thrilled.

"Patty had her moments. On occasion, she would strike out and try to bite you. I hate to bring this up to some of you who might not have seen that particular behavior. People who took care of her during her life knew that when her medication wasn't quite right, that's when her temperament would change dramatically and she could be pretty ornery to everybody but me. I've been trying for years and years and years to get family members to listen to Patty about what a wonderful guy I am, to no avail! Most of the time, Patty was a very happy, enthusiastic, bubbly person, which always was remarkable to me because of her limitations and what most of us expect out of life. She really appreciated everything in life, even the very little things.

"In 1958, when Patty had her first serious breakdown, she talked non-stop for a week. The doctors indicated that the continual internal struggle with observing her siblings, Kathy, myself, and Colleen, going about our daily lives finally got to her, finally had a major impact on her and she had a nervous breakdown. She was institutionalized for the first time in her life in Camarillo State Hospital, about 50 miles north of Los Angeles, where she remained for nine years. Camarillo State Hospital was not a pretty place but it was the only option available at that time in that part of the state.

"From there, Patty moved to Idaho, lived briefly at home with Mom and Dad in Twin Falls, then into several institutional settings, and finally a nursing home in Pocatello when our parents moved there. When Mom and Dad eventually moved back to Twin Falls, Patty also returned where she resided in a nursing home.

"In 1997, Patty moved to the BMW Main Street House in Jerome and enjoyed a lifestyle that amazed us all. Her quality of life was just so superior to anything she'd had since her younger days when she'd lived at home. For our family, one of our constant frustrations was what could we do to make Patty's life better? It was a frustration to me for most of her life until she moved to the Main Street House.

"All of a sudden, Patty was going bowling, she was going swimming at Sligars. This girl was running all over. They kept her busy with a variety of different activities. It was terrific! We are so thankful to Marla and all the staff at the BMW House in Jerome. We are deeply indebted to them and forever grateful for what they did for Patty. These are remarkable people! I know they are not appreciated to the extent that they should be.

"There are many people who were important in Patty's life. Our Uncle Jack Mitchell, my Mother's brother, lived in southern California, had a little three-acre ranch in West Covina years ago and was a true unforgettable character! I don't remember ever going to his home when Uncle Jack had anything on but a swimsuit. He was a large man with a substantial mid-section and didn't look that great in a swimsuit, but that was his preferred attire. He always called Patty "Patsy Murphy". Where he came up with that, I'm not sure. He always had a big smile on his face and he'd say to her, "Patsy Murphy, how are you, dear?" He was just crazy about Patty, but then so many, many people were.

"Another friend not only of Patty's, but of the entire family's, was Joe Champommiere and his wife, Clare. My Dad was a stonemason and Joe was his partner. People would tend to just light up when they'd see Patty and so would she and maybe that's why they reacted that way. Joe and Clare had that kind of reaction to Patty. Clare was an amazing woman who took in over 100 foster children in her long life, and she and Joe took care of Patty more than once when Mother was sick and they loved her to death.

"Joe Rauser was a strange and interesting part of Patty's life. Joe was a classmate of mine at Serra High School in Gardena, California, from 1954 to 1958. He graduated from Serra and went into the seminary to become a priest. I'm not really sure how much of a friendship he and Patty had. He came to the house on a few occasions but anytime Patty would have a little spell, she would want us to get in touch with Joe Rauser. I think Patty had a fantasy love affair with Joe Rauser for over 40 years. It was just one of those interesting little quirks of Patty's that whenever she'd go off on a tangent, Joe Rauser's name would come up. Actually, I don't think anyone in the family had any contact with Joe from about 1959 on.

"Our dear friends, Stasia and Jean Barry, lived in Hawthorne right around the corner from us on Ocean Gate Avenue. We've been close with Stasia and Jean and their kids for over fifty years now. Stasia has just been an incredible friend to Patty. She's not a relative but through the years she has never forgotten Patty and continued to visit her on a regular basis. Patty was just crazy about Stasia! She will always be an important part of our family.

"Mother and Dad pretty much sacrificed their lives for Patty. Mother carried more of the burden of that on a daily basis. Mother and Patty had a wonderfully close relationship that changed over time. As Mother got older, Patty was scolding her!

"Kathy and Colleen have been incredible in their devotion to Patty, and unbelievably loyal in taking care of her. Sheryl and I have been in Boise for sixteen years so I haven't been as close to Patty as they have been. It didn't seem to bother her a bit. I was still number one on her list. Her sisters would be taking care of Patty, seeing her on a weekly basis, and I'm up in Boise, coming down to visit once every two or three months, but she would get irritated with them and chew them out for one thing or another while, of course, I was just wonderful.

"Patty and I were very close. Many people think that a handicapped person is fortunate to have loving and attentive people in his or her family, but those of us who live with a handicapped person in our lives know that we are the lucky ones. Patty had a tremendous impact on all of our lives and we were the ones that were fortunate in that relationship.

"There are many different views of what heaven might be like. We all hope and pray that it is a place where Patty will be able to throw away her wheelchair and run and jump for the first time. If that's the case, Mother and Dad's lives would be complete."

I'M FREE

Don't grieve for me, for now I'm free.
I'm following the path God laid for me.
I took his hand when I heard him call,
I turned my back and left it all.
I could not stay another day,
To Laugh, to love, to work or play.
Tasks left undone must stay that way,
I found peace at close of day.
If my parting has left a void,
Then fill it with remembered joy.
A friendship shared, a laugh, a kiss.
Ah yes, these things, I too, will miss.
Be not burdened with times of sorrow,
I wish you sunshine tomorrow.
My life's been full. I've savored much.
Good friends, good times, a loved one's touch.
Perhaps my time seemed all too brief.
Don't lengthen it now with undue grief.
Lift up your hearts and share with me,
God wanted me now, He set me free.

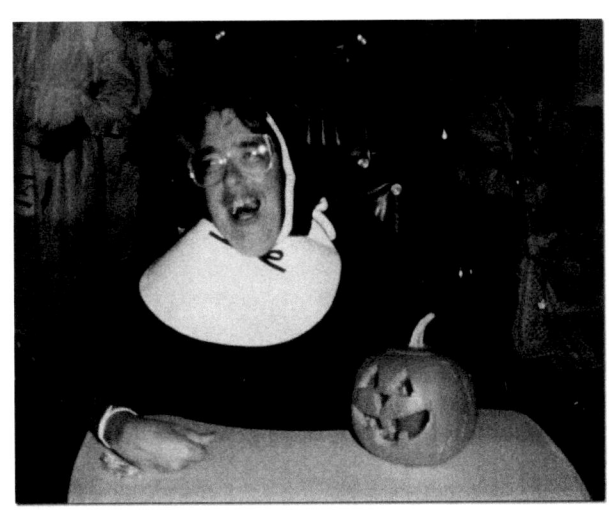

Patty in her favorite Halloween costume, 1994

Bibliography

We consulted a few books and magazine articles in our research and we gratefully acknowledge the following works:

David J. Maklowitz, 2002. *The Bi-Polar Disorder Survival Guide*
Chapter 1, page 7 Bantam Books
New York, New York

Patty Duke, 1992. *A Brilliant Madness*
Chapter 3, page 64 Bantam Books
New York, New York

Bessie Wright, 1999. *The Right Poems*
Chapter 5, page 285 Self-Published

Kay Redfield Jamison, 1995. *An Unquiet Mind*
Part IV, page 211. Alfred A. Knopf Inc.
New York, New York

Professor Rufus J. Fears, 2001 *Churchill*
Lecture 11, The Teaching Company's Great Courses
Chantilly, Virginia

Wikipedia. History of Lithium Pharmacology
Chapter 1

Leo Buscaglia, 1986. *Bus 9 to Paradise*
Chapter, A Passion for Forgiving, page 136 & 137
Slack, Incorporated
Thorofare, New Jersey

Dr. Max Fink, 1999. *Electroshock: Restoring the Mind*
Chapter 1, page 1 Oxford University Press
New York, New York

Dr. Max Fink, 1999. *Electroshock : Restoring the Mind*
Chapter 6, page 52 Oxford University Press
New York, New York

Dr. Max Fink, 1999 *Electroshock : Restoring the Mind*
Chapter 6, page 53 Oxford University Press
New York, New York

Kay Redfield Jamison, 1995. *An Unquiet Mind*
Chapter " They Tell Me It Rained" page 161 & 162
Vintage Books, a division of Random House
New York, New York

About the Authors

Michael J. Thornton has been a realtor in Boise for the past 17 years. He and his wife Sheryl have been married for 47 years and have five children, eleven grandchildren and two great-grandchildren. Michael is also a motivational speaker focusing on family relationships.
Contact him at www. Fitness-over-50.com or 208-861-8000.

Kathleen Thornton Crow was born and raised in Southern California. She has been a resident of Twin Falls, Idaho since her marriage to Bill Crow in 1961. She worked part-time for Bill's Intermountain Bean Co. for 23 years but considers herself fortunate to have been able to devote most of her adult life to the roles of wife, mother and grandmother. Kathy and Bill specialize in girls and have been blessed with three daughters and four granddaughters.